BUILDING
-OTHERS-
UP

Communicating with IMPACT

A Christian Perspective
Of Communication

Abiodun Fijabi

CHURCH
ENVISIONED
INTERNATIONAL

LEADERSHIP · EVANGELISM · TRANSFORMED SOCIETY

Published by: Church Envisioned International | info@cei.org

BUILDING OTHERS UP

Printed in Nigeria by: tt | realitiz & treasures ltd. | +234 805 656 5068, +234 909 548 6070 | tobocy@yahoo.com

DEDICATION

To Dad
You inspired this without knowing.

CONTENTS

ACKNOWLEDGEMENTS

This is a book long in the works. As expected, it has the footprints of many, too numerous to mention here. The list starts with God, the Communicator-In-Chief. You have always had my back. I have stopped wondering why you love me so much. I am satisfied with just enjoying it.

They include teachers and colleagues in many continents. They all share in the glory of its release, while I retain the responsibility for any thumbs downs the book may have.

I bless the day I stumbled on an interview in which a former American President regretted not having taken public speaking seriously in High School. That experience made me commit to improving my communication skills, even as a student of Engineering Science at the University of Ife [Now, Obafemi Awolowo Univeristy, Ile-Ife, Nigeria].

I am grateful to the Evangelical Christian Union [ECU], the Lagos Varsity Christian Union [LVCU] and the Full Gospel Business Men's Fellowship International,, Nigeria [FGBMFI] for providing me platforms to hone my speaking skills.

The Haggai Institute family should take a huge credit for this. This book got a big booster when Dr. Edmund Haggai - the Founder - validated my communication skills. Professor Jeyakar Chellaraj showed me how to communicate, while Professor Arthur Dhanaraj, Dr. David Wong and Dr. Richard Bowie taught me how to teach it. Dr. Beverly Y. Upton-led Haggai Institute's confidence in my facilitation skills has continued to provide me the platform to transfer communication skills to credentialed leaders from across the world.

My research assistants and proofreaders did an excellent job. Thank you, Tobi and Jide. I owe you a lot. Jeremiah Adediran; you were there when I needed you most. I look forward to a payback time. Joshua Praise; I am still wondering if you are human or an angel. Tobore Omogor; this is you at your best. Thank you.

Growing up, my late dad and my mom decided, against all odds, to give me quality education. This book is a result of your inspired decision. My older cousin - Mrs Arinlade Kolapo – I hope you can identify your footprints in the pages. I wrote the first draft of this book in the home of Akin and Tope Akintoye in California. I love you guys. My brother – Abidemi and sisters – Iyabo and Omotayo and your spouses; you are the best support any writer could have. Thank you.

Toluwanimi, you are a daughter like no other. Against your protestations, I have not stopped citing you in my numerous anecdotes and communication examples, as I speak across the world. I hope you will continue to forgive your dad, as I am not likely to stop 'sinning'.

It's almost certain for writers to thank their spouses. I wish to differ. I figure that thanks are not enough for the skinny girl I married in 1988, and who has endured my numerous absences from home to speak and my many tiptoes from the bed at night to write. She is remembered as the wife who said, "Keep writing, honey. Someday, the world will read you." No thanks to you, Mopelola. Instead, I pledge my loyalty and promise lots of love. If these are not enough, I pledge my life.

To my reader, thank you for picking up a copy. I hope it's worth your time and money.

Abiodun Fijabi
Abeokuta
2017

" Do not let any unwholesome talk come out of your mouths, but only what is helpful for building others up according to their needs, that it may benefit those who listen." [NIV]

"Watch the way you talk. Let nothing foul or dirty come out of your mouth. Say only what helps, each word a gift." [MSG]

"Do not use harmful words, but only helpful words, the kind that build up and provide what is needed, so that what you say will do good to those who hear you." [GNT]

Colossians 4:6

"Be gracious in your speech. The goal is to bring out the best in others in a conversation, not put them down, not cut them out." [MSG]

"Let your conversation be always full of grace, seasoned with salt,so that you may know how to answer everyone." [NIV]

WHAT SPEECH IS THIS?

> *"On the Sabbath he began to teach in the synagogue. Many people were there; and when they heard him, they were all amazed. "Where did he get all this?" they asked. "What wisdom is this that has been given him?" Mark 6:2*

I can picture the gathering. Throngs of people packed in the synagogue. Every seat was taken. It was a Sabbath day. A young man, who had been making some stupendous claims, was part of the crowd of worshippers. In a few minutes, he stood up to read the Scriptures and say a few words. He walked briskly to the front. Nothing in his steps or dressing predicted what was about to happen.

He started.

His words were pungent. He spoke persuasively and authoritatively. From his words and the passion he packed into them, it was obvious he had a heart for the people. His love for his hearers oozed out of every word. Men and women sat enraptured. Those who had wanted to leave earlier abandoned the idea. Those who were engaged in side talk switched over and gave this young speaker their attention. There was a deafening silence. No one wanted to miss out a word of his speech. Even though he was challenging their traditions; even though he was asking them to do things differently; even though he was claiming a relationship with Jehovah that was considered sacrilegious, he still had their attention. Some of them could not believe why they were so bought over by the words of this man. His teaching contradicted some of their widely held traditions. But none voiced out their dissent. As if a word spoken, even under their breath, could interrupt the speaker. No one went out. Not even to visit the toilet or pamper a crying child.

The man had just finished.

He took his seat, as if he had done nothing extraordinary – his humility matched only by his speechmaking prowess. Many seconds after, no one moved. No one said anything. Amazement filled their faces. Some mouths stayed open. Some shook their heads in unbelief. Some others wondered in low tones, under their breath. When they finally spoke, the words flowed in torrents.

"Did you hear what I heard?

"No man has spoken with so much authority…"

"So much audacity!"

"Just imagine the way he weaved his words."

'There was nothing he said that we could not identify with."

"He started from what we knew to what he wanted us to know."

"He used the Prophets to back up his message."

"He quoted from the Scriptures as if he wrote them."

"He said, David testified of him."

"I love David so much. I can't love this man less."

"Did you notice how he chastised us and still we listened?"

"He loves us, no doubt. I saw that in his face and read that in his words."

"But it is difficult to do what he said. It will mean abandoning our old traditions."

"He was so persuasive that I am reconsidering my opposition to his message."

"You can disagree with him but you can't resist his words."

"Can someone tell me if what I had just seen and heard was a dream?

"What wisdom is this?"

"What speech is this?"

Effective speechmaking was the hallmark of Jesus' life and ministry. Whether it was when he spoke to a crowd like the above experience or when he spoke one-on-one to the woman at the well, Jesus showed a mastery of words and displayed effective communication skills that impacted his hearers.

Jesus never communicated with two people exactly the same way. To Jesus, the message of the Kingdom was contextual, adaptable to fit into any situation. He related to his audiences. He identified their needs and met them expertly. In furtherance of his incarnation, he broke barriers upon barriers in order to communicate with man. He was divine, but he projected his humanity before us. He could have been distant, but he chose proximity. Being divine, he could have been beyond man's touch. But they touched him and he wasn't insulted. They milled round him; he didn't forbid them. He had no unsmiling bouncers standing between him and the people. And on occasions when his over reaching disciples decided to shield him from the people, he rebuked them openly. He never used high-sounding multi-syllabic words that only impressed his audience. He was out to impact, not to impress. Not everyone accepted his message; he didn't expect them to. But none was indifferent.

Building Others Up

The Jesus-style communication is contrary to our day-to-day experience. The reality shows on cable and television have done little to make our communication impactful. We scream with joy when a contestant is fired or ejected on a show. We watch with excitement as a contestant is told he doesn't measure up to the standards. It is not just what the judges say to them but the way they say it. Brutal words meant to pull down and not to build up. Some contestants cry in agony. Their cry is our own entertainment.

The Church hasn't feared better either.

Imagine Jesus in our church today. Imagine him seated in the back watching the way we address ourselves. He would shudder at the arrogance of the communication coming from the pulpit. He would wonder at the rationale behind the yawning respect gap between the pulpit and the pew. He would watch with indignation as we accord the speaker more attention and give him more consideration than the listener. "You didn't learn that from me; did you?" He would have challenged us. "I broke many barriers to be with people. You have created many more to differentiate yourself from people."

Silently, he would watch as we take ourselves down at home and at work. He would watch the husband and wife competing to cut each other to size. Winning is all that matters, he would observe. He would see the war zone we call the marketplace. He would wonder at the lack of respect for each other in the way we speak and relate. He would regret creating the tongue.

As he moves around in our communities, he would observe the way we have re-written the gospel message and the poor communication of what he originally designed as the power of God unto salvation. He would be alarmed that it is no longer the gospel of the Kingdom but the gospel of convenience. He would see much piety and less righteousness.

He would weep.

That must be what Paul had in mind when he wrote

Ephesians 4:29. He asserted that communication is to benefit a listener. He, the listener, is the reason for biblical communication. Much like the hero of a movie or the centerpiece of a creative design. He is not part of the deal; he is the real deal. That's why he suggests that the speaker concentrates on building others up according to their needs. Yes, you read that right. *Building others up.* According to Paul, any communication that is not designed to build others up is 'harmful', 'dirty' and 'unwholesome'.

Does anyone wonder why we are not impacting our world? There can be no impact without building up. Our words would continue to lack the power to affect our generation as long as they are harmful, dirty and unwholesome. As a Church, our impact on the world would be curtailed without it. Our family life would suffer irreparably without it. Our workplace and communities would suffer further degradation without it. It is build up or perish.

There can be no hope for our world without quality communication, the type that the Bible recommends.

02

COMMUNICATION IS IT!

Many years ago, Coca Cola Company ran an impressive campaign that took the world by storm. The advert was short and terse: *Coca Cola is it!* It left you to define the question and describe your situation. But whatever the question or situation, there was only one answer – Coke. Not many believed it, but they drank Coke anyway. As many people drank coke, the company smiled to its bank.

I am persuaded Communication, not Coke, is it. What in our world can survive without communication? Certainly, not any of our institutions - Education, family, and government are some of the vital institutions around which our lives revolve. None of them exists without communication. In fact, each of them requires effective communication for continued relevance.

What happened to relationships – the building block of any community? How can two people work together except they have a form of agreement? And how can they reach an agreement without communication? Relationships falter without communication. And with faltering relationships come the crumbling of the community.

Ever thought of what becomes of leadership without communication? Leadership is the engine room for change, progress and development in any society. It thrives on vision. A vision that is not shared and effectively too will soon be consigned to the dustbin of history. It stands no chance of survival let alone create an attractive future. Now, sharing is communication. Vision dies without communication and with it leadership and our hope of a better and progressive society.

Perhaps what seals our hope of any form of existence without communication is our inability to get the Gospel message across to the needy world. The Gospel remains the only hope of the world. The preaching of the Gospel to the whole world is Jesus' last command but our first priority as Christians. But how can the Gospel be preached without a preacher? And how can there be a preacher without communication?

It is inconceivable to think of a world without communication. Such a situation would make the confusion in the aftermath of the Tower of Babel pale into insignificance. Hope would dim. Life would come to a halt. It would be an unmitigated disaster.

God is Communication

At the beginning of this book, we saw Jesus communicating with impact. We might be tempted to think that God waited till the arrival of his Son before he showed us quality communication. That would be further from the truth.

God started communicating with humanity from the very beginning. Communication is not the invention of the human mind. God was there at the beginning shaping the world by his word. The Bible opened with the story of the God that worked. He rolled up his sleeves and went to work on his disordered world. How did God work? Did he take the hammer and the chisel? Did he run down the dark and void world with earthmoving equipment? Did he use a crane to reach the high points of his creation?

God spoke. In speaking, he worked. That is a fact our world is yet to grapple with - The fact that communication is work. It is a creative and perspiring human endeavour.

Let us try and get the picture right. God, in the beginning, created the heaven and the earth. Then things went awry, as they sometimes do. The earth was without form and void. On top of that, darkness ruled the earth. Then, God started to speak. As he spoke, the creation listened and obeyed. The result was a recreated world.

What are we saying here? Once, God's world was endangered. It was formless, void and dark. The truine challenge called for God's concerted action. No kid-glove treatment would surfice. God's plan to create an abode for humans who would carry out his plans on earth was in jeorpardy. As expected, God did not fret. The God of heaven and earth would not shrink before any challenge, no matter its proportion. He also did not fold his arms. He acted and concertedly too. But what he did was unexpected.

He spoke.

Perhaps we would not have been surprised if he had evolved a brilliant idea to restore his disordered world. A project idea – well conceived and well implemented would have been consistent with his divine character as the God of vision.

But God simply spoke. This is not to mean that ideas are not vital but God had chosen to speak. As he spoke, his words reverberated through the entire earth – creating form, filling the void and lightening the darkness. It took him six days.

God has not stopped speaking since then.

> *"How clearly the sky reveals God's glory! How plainly it shows what he has done! Each day announces it to the following day; each night repeats it to the next. No speech or words are used, no sound is heard; yet their message goes out to all the world and is heard to the ends of the earth..." Psalm 19:1-4 [GNB]*

As the above scripture suggests, God has been speaking

through nature. His creation speaks volumes, attesting to his works and glory. Though no words are uttered, the message still goes forth to the ends of the earth. As we will discover in subsequent chapters, this is a type of communication that is carried out without using words. It is called non-verbal communication.

God has effectively used written communication to reach his creatures – to teach them his precepts and to guide them in their life's endeavours. "Your word is a lamp unto my feet; and a light unto my path." [Psalms. 119:105]. Paul, writing to Timothy, emphasizes the importance of the scriptures as being inspired of God and suitable for "teaching the truth, rebuking error, correcting faults, and giving instruction for right living..." [2 Timothy 3:16]

Why are we so captivated by the Bible? Is it just because it is the word of God? Or also because it is a page-turner? It is a beautiful work of art, providing all the variations to arouse and sustain our interests. There are elements of prose, poem and drama. In the Bible, you will find suspense, comedy, intrigues, stories, illustrations, visual aids and all. We remember the words of the Scriptures because they are attractively packaged. They are not cold words that distract and inhibit communication. We read the scriptures and say wow! In the beauty of those words, we receive inspiration, guidance and help. We are drawn back to it again and again and again. God, through his word – beautifully expressed – has arrested us.

God has been very creative in his communication efforts with man. He has used and still uses the services of angels to get his message across to his people. He has used prophets. He has spoken directly to some either loudly or through the still small voice. Constantly, he speaks to the human spirit through the inner witness.

The task of communication is so important to the Godhead that all the members are involved in this endeavour. The Holy Spirit spoke and still speaks to our generation.

> *"While they were serving the Lord and fasting, the Holy Spirit said to them, "Set apart for me Barnabas and Saul, to do the work to which I have called them." Acts 13:2*

The climax of God's communication with man was through his Son Jesus. The whole idea of incarnation is God's way of identifying with man in order to communicate effectively with him.

> *"In the past God spoke to our ancestors many times and in many ways through the prophets, but in these last days he has spoken to us through his Son. He is the one through whom God created the universe, the one whom God has chosen to possess all things at the end. He reflects the brightness of God's glory and is the exact likeness of God's own being, sustaining the universe with his powerful word." Hebrews 1:1-3*

Jesus epitomizes God's communication with man. He is the medium of God's communication with humanity. Through him, we see God, understand his ways and receive the fullness of his presence. But he does not only show us the way; he is the way. He is not just the medium, he is the message. John captures this graphically when he writes, "In the beginning was the word and the word was with God and the word was God," It is this 'Word" that became flesh and dwelt among us. And it is this Jesus that holds everything together by his powerful words.

> *"...He holds everything together by what he says--powerful words!" Hebrews 1:3* [MSG]

If Jesus holds everything by his powerful words, the world ends up in disarray without communication. The situation in our world will be similar to one described by William Butler Yeats [1865-1939]

Turning and turning in the widening gyre
The falcon cannot hear the falconer;
Things fall apart; the centre cannot hold.
Mere anarchy is loosed upon the world

It is obvious that our God is a communicating God. But beyond being a communicating God, our God is communication, the same way he is love.

The Challenge

Today, the challenge has not been less daunting than it was in the beginning. The Christian leader constantly battles emptiness, formlessness, and social, moral and spiritual darkness. We are faced with challenges of a world that is slipping away from its creator and choosing the path of destruction. We are also faced with a loving

God who is not interested in the death of sinners and a loving Father who wants his recalcitrant children to come back home.

The Christian leader stands in the middle. He lives with two realities. One as defined by his day-to-day experience in the fallen and falling world. And the other defined by the God of the Bible. The Christian leader sees the perversion of all human institutions and shudders. But he also sees a God who is alive and active in the world he created, and he is encouraged. He sees the hopelessness that permeates every human endeavour and feels intimidated. But he also sees the heart of a loving God and is challenged to hope. He sees human defiance and God's terror. He sees human's pain and God's joy. He sees human's propensity for sin and God's unlimited grace.

The mirror before a Christian has two faces.

For those Christians that have the heart of the Father, they cannot but look at the two faces of the same mirror. God is not looking for angels who only see one face of the mirror to change his world. Only the man created in his image fits the bill of his change agents.   Only man is attuned with God and with the world. The world is his abode, his home. It is here he builds a family, engages in a work, finds pleasure and lives in a community. Because of his involvement with his world, he feels its joys and pains. He feels it when the economy booms and when terror strikes. But we will be wrong to limit man to this sphere. There is yet another and more important sphere of existence. It relates to the origin of man. Man has a source – God. He is a spirit being like his creator. That ties him intricately to

God. Based on his decisions, a good relationship develops between him and his God. Like two friends, they can share information on the spheres of man's existence on which they both have interests. So, sharing God's passion is possible and feeling his heartbeat plausible.

Do you now understand the reason behind incarnation? Jesus as the Son shares the heart of his Father but he has to become a man to feel the human pulse. That is what qualifies him. That is what qualifies us.

A Christian therefore becomes a bridge between God and the world. Indeed, the Bible says he is. As an ambassador of Christ, he represents Christ in a world that he lives in, not as an on-looker but as an active participant. To do this effectively, the Bible asserts the Christian has the word of reconciliation. Meaning that communication will play a vital role in man's attempt to present God to man and bring man back to God.

In essence, victory in serving as ambassadors lies in effective communication. Like it was at the beginning, so it is now. Formlessness and emptiness are threatening our world. So is darkness that has covered the earth wondering if light would ever shine. We stand no chance of winning the war if we adopt a method different from the one God used. God spoke. God communicated. We also must speak. We also must communicate with the hurting world. Only effective communication fills the void in our lopsided world, provides form and shape to a society without Godly values and represents the other side of darkness – light.

Now, its time to ignite your vocal chord and speak. But wait a minute…

Our Report Card

Before you ignite your vocal chord, you need to know how we humans have used and have been using words. You probably know by now that we are not doing too well. But may be you really do not know how bad the situation is. Most of our communication efforts fail. Some experts say seven out of every ten human efforts at communicating fail.

That is not the kind of report card you will condone from your child. That is not the kind of performance you will applaud. But human beings are not known to do only the reasonable, as you will discover later in this chapter.

The cost of ineffective communication is enormous. A husband is persuaded he loves his wife. He sets out to convey this to his wife. But what his wife hears is how much he hates her. A teacher has one goal – to get his students to pass an external examination. The results are out and majority of the students fail to make the pass mark. A leader has a vision – to mobilize his fast growing church to agree to a church extension. He speaks with deep conviction but the church votes down his proposal. An evangelist knows his message like the back of his hand. His compassion for the lost has never been in doubt. He is persuaded he has a message that can change lives. He shares this message and no one responds.

All these and many more happen around us constantly and we are not mourning. It is convenient to put the problem at the feet of the listeners. The teacher blames the students for not being studious enough. The husband blames the wife for distorting his message. The leader slams down the parishioners for being so short-sighted. The evangelist blames the failure in getting the message across on the spirit of the times.

We blame everyone except the speaker for the failure of our communication efforts. We cannot be more wrong. As we will find out; the responsibility of getting the message across rests more with the speaker than with the listener.

The importance of communication is more evident when we realize that we communicate all the time. Experts say, we communicate in one form or another seventy percent of the time. You communicate each time you think, reflect, meditate or soliloquize. Even our silence is a form of communication. And whereas your voice may be disengaged, your body language continues the communication. If this is an endeavour we do more than any other, then the high failure rate in communication should be a serious concern to both the Christian leader and the evangelist.

The Bible recognizes the challenge of communication when it uses it as the yardstick for measuring perfection. *"We all stumble in many ways. Anyone who is never at fault in what they say is perfect, able to keep their whole body in check."* *[James 3:2]*

It would look like this is one thing we *must* get right to be effective in our leadership and evangelistic endeavours.

Why The Dismal Failure?

The truth is, as some experts have observed, *"One cannot not communicate."*
Communication is as vital to man as his breath. You define the problem and name the situation; one endeavour stands out from all other human endeavours. You might just say; Communication is it!

Yet, the importance of communication is yet to dawn on many in our world, especially on the men and women who have been given the responsibility of reconciling the hurting world with God, the creator. Ignorance breeds ineptitude. Ineptitude sinks us deeper in communication failure. Our message then loses its potency and the world is left to consider other options. When non-believers say they love our Christ but can't stick to us, Christians, they are reminding us how deep we have sunk in our effort at communicating with them.

One can hardly imagine why ignorance persists with the overwhelming evidence of that makes effective communication inevitable. We mourn many other losses, but we fail to count our losses in communication. For example, the passing of loved ones to eternity is considered a huge loss. Suddenly, the one we love is no more. Most cultures of the world believe it is appropriate to mourn the dead. We do this in a variety of ways. We mourn the dead but are oblivious of the great obituary of failed communication all around us. The fact that we bury seven out of every ten words we speak means no much to us. It is a tragedy.

If ignorance has bred ineptitude, poor attitude has crippled our effort at changing the way we communicate with the hurting world.

Dr. Edmund Haggai captures this eloquently when he wrote: "Effective speaking is both an art and a science. It is an art, requiring the same earnest attention, persistent practice and careful technique as the mastery of painting, sculpture or music. It is a science based on the laws of psychology."

If communication is an art, then it lends itself to techniques that can be learnt through persistent and disciplined practice. If it is an art, it is a creative endeavour that comes from skills acquired over time. There is an element of romance in art. There is some emotional attachment that the artist develops for his works that keeps him going.

If communication is a science, then it is a precise body of knowledge that is based on introverted laws of nature. In this case, the laws of psychology and of human impression. These laws can then be researched, learned and applied like the laws of physics or chemistry. These laws apply whether we believe them or not. A man who falls from a sixteen floor building because he does not believe in the laws of gravity will nevertheless be subject to the law of gravity. He pays dearly for his ignorance. The same applies to the laws of psychology as in public speaking. You break the law; you face the consequence. You obey the law; you experience the predicted outcome.

How many Christian leaders have had training in communication? Most will consider it unnecessary. To most believers, speaking comes naturally and requires no formal training. Some passages of the Scriptures have been used to support the thinking that speaking – whether in public or private – should be left to the Holy Spirit. Let us consider here a few of them.

> *"For Christ did not send me to baptize, but to preach the gospel—not with wisdom and eloquence, lest the cross of Christ be emptied of its power." 1 Corinthians 1:17*

> *"And so it was with me, brothers and sisters. When I came to you, I did not come with eloquence or human wisdom as I proclaimed to you the testimony about God." 1 Corinthians 2:1*

> *"My message and my preaching were not with wise and persuasive words, but with a demonstration of the Spirit's power," 1 Corinthians 2:4*

> *"But when they arrest you, do not worry about what to say or how to say it. At that time you will be given what to say," Matthew 10:19*

Three issues are involved here, in my opinion. The first is the issue of 'enticing words'. These are words that are calculated to take advantage of the listener. They are words without integrity. As you will find out, integrity is a vital pillar of effective communication. The second issue has to do with 'human wisdom'. We all can easily identify with this. We call it 'secular wisdom' – a nomenclature I consider abnormal. Human wisdom is not necessarily anti-God. Human wisdom based on natural laws is part of God's truth. Human wisdom that is corrupted is to be avoided. Same with human wisdom that is used exclusive of God. It is similar to a Christian trying to live a holy life by his strength without relying on the power of the Holy Spirit. This is not to say human effort is not entirely needed in holy living. It is the Christian who will "flee from fornication", "speak the truth in love", "run the race with patience", "work out his salvation with fear and trembling", and "take on the whole armour of God", among others.

It is ironic that the same leader that frowns at learning the techniques of public speaking because it is human wisdom encourage years of training in medicine, engineering, philosophy and other fields of human endeavour. There is nothing that makes any of these fields more spiritual than communicating.

Praying for divine protection and running away from an oncoming vehicle are not mutually exclusives. You do not do one and leave the other. No Christian in his right senses will rely only on prayers to have a child without subjecting himself to the laws of biological reproduction. He will rather pray and at the same time do what he has to do with his wife.

The third issue, I believe, has to do with 'taking thought of what to say and how to say it'. Of course, thinking about what to say and how to say it is an important ingredient of effective communication. The context here is similar to what is usually referred to as 'thinking on your feet'. The prescription of God is perfect. People who think on their feet do not struggle to get words out. They simply stand before the audience with confidence that the right words will come out. And this is not achieved in a vacuum. This confidence comes through previous preparations. It is for the speaker that is "…always…prepared to give an answer to everyone who asks you to give the reason for the hope that you have." [1 Peter 3:15]

The Christian leader needs to change his attitude about communication being entirely an act of the Holy Spirit. The truth is that effective speech making based on skill and on laws of psychology is not at variance with the reliance on the Holy Spirit. He does not need to choose one and leave the other. Both are essential to the success of his communication endeavour. The Christian does his part and the Holy Spirit does his.

With the desire to learn and with the right attitudes, we can stem the tide of the great communication obituary that has pervaded our world and restricted our level of impact as believers.

CHAPTER

03

TALK IS CHEAP

A telecommunication company has as a catchphrase; *Say what you want to say.* With that the company hopes to get everyone talking as it smiles to its bank. Yet another communication company eager to sell its services tells the public, *Talk is cheap.* It encourages its subscribers to take advantage of its lower rates to talk endlessly. With that, the company hopes to keep its network busy and its business booming.

The problem is not that we are not talking. We, in fact, talk a lot. Talking is the human activity we do more than any other. But the question is, 'Are we talking right?' Or, if you like, are we communicating? In one way or the other, we send messages to non-believers about Jesus. But are those messages clear? Are they understood in the form we intend? Are they persuasive enough to make the non-Christian respond positively to the message?

The word *Communicate* comes from the Latin word, *Communicare*, meaning, 'to impart' or 'to participate'. The root word of the Latin word, *Communicare* is *Communis*, meaning, 'to make common'.

The implications of these are obvious – Communication is not what we thought it was. It is not a mere expression of thoughts, ideas or information. It is a desire to impart. According to Dictionary.com, to impart means 'to make known; tell; relate; disclose; to give; to bestow." Impartation is not complete until the message has been made known in the form intended. In imparting you relate; meaning that communication is not a solo effort. If you cannot barb a man's head without his permission, you certainly cannot impart him without his cooperation. Until someone has received your gift, you have not given it. Until a message is understood, as you wanted it to be, you have not bestowed it.

Communication also means; *to participate*. Again, Dictionary.com comes to the rescue. It defines participate as; 'to take or have a part or share, as with others; partake; share.' This means both the speaker and the listener have a part or a share in the message. They have a stake in the message and in the process in which it is conveyed. To participate also means, according Merriam-Webster, '*to possess some of the attributes of a person, thing, or quality'*. That is, beyond having a stake in the message and the process of conveying it, the speaker must possess some of the attributes or qualities of the audience. The speaker is expected to understand and adapt to the listener in such a way that he assumes some of the listener's characteristics for effective participation.

Now, it should be obvious communication is not what we thought it was. But wait until we consider another root word, *Communis*, meaning, 'to make common.' Making the message common to both parties is the hallmark of effective communication. The goal of a Christian witness is to help the non-Christian come to a common understanding with him. This requires building common grounds and removing obstacles that might impede common meaning. The extent to which both of them attain common experience (commonality) regarding the content and the meaning of the message determines the level of effectiveness of their communication.

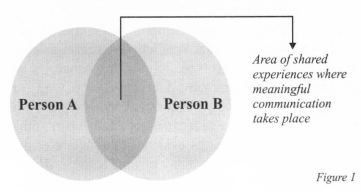

Area of shared experiences where meaningful communication takes place

Person A   **Person B**

Figure 1

Wilbur Schramm's Simple Diagram of Overlapping Circles

As the above diagram shows, communication takes place only where there are shared experiences. Since experiencing commonality is vital to effective communication, the speaker's empathy for the listener becomes imperative. An effective speaker is concerned about the feelings and the circumstances of the listener and seeks to know as much about the listener as possible to allow the building of common grounds.

I hope you have concluded communication is not a piece of cake. It is not as easy as A, B, C. It is a lot of work and requires so much more than most communicators are willing to invest in it.

So, What Is Communication?

There are as many definitions of communication as there are communication experts. However, the essential of communication is the **mutual** exchange of **information** and **understanding** between the speaker and the audience by any **effective** means.

If communication is mutual, then it is not a solo effort. For communication to be effective, both the speaker and the audience must be involved. It is an exchange. If an exchange, then the communicator is not satisfied with just having information but is also concerned about how to transfer it. This comes with experience on the part of the speaker and the listener as evident in the failure of the Nigerian 4 X 100 meters relay quartet at the 2003 All African Games in Abuja, Nigeria. Prior to the games, Nigerian sprinters were in top form, putting up superlative performances at International meets. No one would consider putting a bet against the Nigerian quartet, more so, when Nigeria won most of the medals in the sprints before the relay quartets went on the starting blocks. The relay was won by the Ghanaian quartet. They won it because their exchange of batons were near perfect. Unlike the individually skilled Nigerian team that was hurriedly put together, the Ghanaian team had been training together for many years.

For effective communication, both parties, and especially the communicator, need to develop exchange skills. Communication involves an exchange. It involves the transferring of experiences to listeners by the sender so that they (the listeners) can also have the same experiences. Individual skill is vital but communication is a team sport. It is transactional. It is a relationship.

You might say there can be no communication without a message and you will be right. Information represents the ideas, the thoughts, opinions or the experiences that the communicator plans to transfer to the listener. Experience in this context refers to knowledge of concepts, theories, ideas, facts...acquired by the sender through listening, reading, studying, experimenting, reflecting and experiencing. The romance of the communicator with the message is essential in a communication process. The information must be experiential to the communicator before he can transfer it confidently and effectively. The disciples of Jesus were able to saturate their world with the gospel because as John said, "That which was from the beginning, which we have heard, which we have seen with our eyes, which we have looked at and our hands have touched—this we proclaim concerning the Word of life." I John 1:1

The use of 'effective means' makes it mandatory on the speaker to identify the best out of the approaches available to him, to get his message across. This requires that the speaker research the listener and the best approaches to ensure mutual understanding between him and the speaker. It places the responsibility of getting the message across to the speaker and not to the listener.

It should now be more obvious therefore that communication is not as simple as it seems. To be sure, communication is not just simply igniting your vocal chord. It is not mere speaking. It is a hard work. But it is a task that must be done if you desire to make the difference in your generation. You should now understand why Jesus looked at the bountiful harvest and bemoaned the scarcity of labourers.

> *"He told them, "The harvest is plentiful, but the workers are few. Ask the Lord of the harvest, therefore, to send out workers into his harvest field." Luke 10:2*

There may be many pretending to be labourers and whose words carry no power. They speak but their words touch no lives. They fail to reach out to the hurting world effectively because they are doing everything else except to communicate. They lose out on the opportunity to become an agent of change.

Why Do We Communicate?

A communicator desires to be understood. He has a message, which he wants the listener to understand the same way that he (the speaker) understands it. To do this effectively, the speaker must understand the listener first. Every speaker loses the right to be heard and understood until he has sought to hear and understand the listener first.

The essence of communication, as many communication experts have observed, is to seek to understand first and then to be understood. This runs against the grain of many communication efforts which only seek to bundle their ideas and information on the listener without first understanding the need and the peculiarities of the listener.

The ultimate purpose of communication is to evoke action from the listener based on his understanding of the shared information and ideas. There is a shift in understanding. The listener is better informed than before the communication experience. His response or action based on the new understanding represents change. Change does not always have to be physical as in giving to the church's project or indicating readiness to make Jesus the Lord of their lives. Sometimes, change is attitudinal. The listener may have changed his opinion about tithing or giving. Or he may have accepted that women are to be treated with great respect. Change may be subtle or pronounced. The non-Christian that weeps openly for his sin is experiencing change. The same may be true of another whose head is bowed in quiet solitude, pondering on his ways and seeking to make amends. Regardless of nature and significance, change is inevitable in any effective communication experience.

Why do we need to change people's attitudes and behaviour through communication? Primarily because we are at different levels of development based on our differing experiences and we need to constantly share our experiences for mutual development and harmony. The future of our society is hinged on constant change arising from new and progressive experiences. The sharing of these experiences by those who have them brings the much needed societal transformation and development. Besides, there is the need to acquire new experiences for personal growth and transformation. A man that stops changing stops living.

As desirable as change is, human beings do everything possible to resist it. Change makes us susceptible to vulnerability. It often removes us from the familiar terrain, from our comfort zone. Fear that the new experience might fail is real and formidable. In the process of evoking change, the communicator has to battle against this resistance. Experienced communicators recognize this resistance and how it might rob them of success in their communication effort. That is why they adapt appropriate approach and depend on the Holy Spirit to help them break the listener's resistance to change.

The Bible On Communication

The Bible concurs with the need to be listener-focused in our desire to change [or build others up] through communication.

> *"Do not let any unwholesome talk come out of your mouths, but only what is helpful for building others up according to their needs, that it may benefit those who listen." Ephesians 4: 29*

We might think only the use of foul and 'unchristian' language constitutes 'unwholesome talk'. We are dead wrong. Our language can be full of Christian jargons and still be unwholesome. The Biblical yardstick is not so much with the language as with the effect. What does your speech achieve? Does it build up or does it pull down the listener? Is the listener better off after the communication than before it? Even if the listener does not agree with you, has he nevertheless moved up on the ladder of understanding of the gospel?

You might ask, how do you build up non-Christians? The Bible answers unambiguously, "according to their needs". That is awesome. The non-Christian needs come into play. Their needs come to the center stage. Suddenly, the presenter of the Good News becomes an adventurous caregiver. He knows he can't go anywhere without first understanding the needs of his listener. He knows if he stumbles at understanding the needs of the listener, he stumbles at the task of communicating the Good News to him. So, he ponders at this important bus stop. He elicits the power of the Holy Spirit, who knows all things and who carries a passion of the Trinity to have "all men saved and come to the knowledge of the truth". He submits to the Teacher who has been sent "to teach us all things and show us things to come." And so, he listens as the non-Christian speaks of his travails, of his hopes, and of his beliefs. He ponders on those words, seeking to understand the listener and fashioning the appropriate and the best means to respond. He is clear-minded about his goal – to build up the non-Christian according to his needs. The purpose of the communication effort is also not lost on him – To benefit the listener.

It is the listener all the way.

The focus of a biblical communication is the listener. Building him up according to his needs is the goal of biblical communication and to benefit him the purpose. To do otherwise is to be guilty of making an unwholesome speech. Now you can begin to imagine how many unwholesome speeches we make in a day.

CHAPTER

YOU COMMUNICATING WITH YOU

Before you say a word to a non-Christian, to your spouse or to your colleague in the office, you have said about three words to yourself. You speak more to yourself than you speak to others. This communication with yourself is called intrapersonal Communication. It is the prelude to your communication with others, called Interpersonal Communication. And as you will discover, intrapersonal communication is the driving force of your Christian witness and communication with other people. Intrapersonal and Interpersonal communication are the two basic ways we engage ourselves in the exchange of information and experiences.

What Are You Saying To You?

Hers was a sorry case. She had had it for twelve years. She had hoped for deliverance with every passing day but none had come. The doctors had made a living out her; so much that she was now penniless. The persistent bleeding had cut her off from life and living. No one wanted to be associated with an outcast. She was unclean, according to tradition. She was exempted from associating with men. Her only companions were shame and pain. Her world had collapsed. But not her faith; she cherished a deep conviction that God could and would bring solution to her problem. That gave her hope. Others saw a woman who was down and out; she saw herself living once more among men and making a vital contribution to the society. Others saw her as a victim, she saw a champion in herself. They saw hopelessness, but she cherished an undying hope.

One day, her time came as it always does for people who believe. Jesus was in her community. The crowd was thick around him. She stood no chance of attracting Jesus' attention. Her voice would be drowned in the ocean of other high pitch voices. Did she give up? No. She spoke to herself. Her intrapersonal communication was all she had. It was her only hope of securing a personal relationship with Jesus and with this relationship her healing.

"She said to herself, "If I only touch his cloak, I will be healed.""Matthew 9:21

Those words flowed through her mind in torrents. She believed what she said to herself and inched her way through the crowd to touch Jesus' cloak. Without saying a word, she communicated interpersonally with Jesus. She secured Jesus' attention in a way many around could not understand. And it all started from speaking to herself.

Peter was a disciple who would not let go easily of his traditional biases. He knew God wanted him to reach out to the gentiles but in the corner of his mind, he could not imagine himself doing so. It was this attitude God wanted to change. To do this, God chose to communicate with him pictorially in a vision. At the end of this captivating vision, Peter decided to do one thing most effective communicators do – reflect on what he had just experienced. It was in the process of reflecting that he heard the Lord say to him that some men were looking for him and that he should follow them without questioning. That empowered his communication with the men and with the household of Cornelius later.

In the cases of the woman and Peter, intrapersonal communication was employed effectively as a preparation to interpersonal communication. While the woman spoke to herself, Peter just reflected on the experience he had just had. What the woman and Peter did was called self-talk. Some call it, soliloquizing. Thinking, meditating, reflecting and soliloquizing are all forms of self-talk or intrapersonal communication. They all describe the huge information flow process that constantly engages your mind. It is the communication you have within yourself. It is you communicating with you. You are probably not aware of this, but you speak to yourself a lot. A research shows you speak to yourself between 400 and 800 words per minute and speak to others between 150 and 250 words a minute. You should now understand why the Bible says, *"For the mouth speaks what the heart is full of." [Matthew 12:24]*

Your communication with others is an outflow of your communication within you. If intrapersonal communication is defective, interpersonal communication is sure to be defective.

How vital is this communication to your efforts at evoking change in your life and in the lives of others? As vital as you can imagine. The Bible says, you are what we think about yourself [Proverbs.23:7].You are the source or the initiator of the communication process. You are crucial to the communication process. If you are as you think, then your thinking enhances or impedes your communication with yourself and with others. That explains why effective communicators are constantly seeking to improve the quality of their self-talk.

Improving Your Self-talk

Christian leaders and evangelists have a responsibility to prepare themselves adequately for effective interpersonal communication by improving the level of their self-talk. They do so in a variety of ways.

- *Inner peace*

One of the ways to do this is to guard jealously their inner peace. Peace is the serenity of mind regardless of the prevailing circumstances. Peace is part of our new creation realities and an inheritance we have in Christ. One of the greatest challenges of anyone, no less of a Christian leader, is maintaining this peace. Issues that seek to frustrate this peace are constantly bombarding us. Anytime we succumb to these pressures, we lose our peace. With the resulting disturbed mind, we are sure candidates for an ineffective communication with others. Effective communicators allow the Lord to deal with issues that confront them. In the end, they do not have fewer challenges but they develop the right attitudes to them. Having sustained this peace, they are ever ready to enter into communication with others.

"Don't worry about anything, but in all your prayers ask God for what you need, always asking him with a thankful heart. And God's peace, which is far beyond human understanding, will keep your hearts and minds safe in union with Christ Jesus." Philippians 4:6-8

With the peace of God, like a garrison of soldiers, guarding our hearts and minds, we cannot fail in communication.

- ## *Self-Esteem*

Have you spoken to a man lately who thinks little of himself? Did you observe any self-confidence in his speech? Did he feel persuaded about his subject? Most importantly, did he persuade you to see his point of view?

The Bible advises against being high-minded. Leaders need to constantly guide against thinking more highly of themselves. But they should not think lowly of themselves either. Healthy self-opinion about our importance is not synonymous with pride. It is our ability to be conscious of who we are in Christ and to resist with all humility every attempt to pull us down. Paul told Timothy not to let anyone despise his youth. He wasn't asking his spiritual son to pick up a quarrel with anyone that sought to despise him. I believe Paul was making a case for a healthy self-opinion. A man with self-esteem does not have to defend himself or respond to an attempt to pull him down. He doesn't have to get angry. He simply believes the best about himself regardless of the way he is received or treated.

- *A purpose for life*

Communication is a life-long endeavour. It is a boring exercise for those without a purpose for living. A clear view of what you are here for instills hope and courage. There is something to live for. There is something to look forward to as the day dawns. There is something to hope for in the midst of despair. There is something to die for when courage is what counts. All these inspire confident speaking.

- *A positive self-talk*

What do you say to yourself more often under your breath? What words run through your mind as you move from one activity to another? When encountered with pain, what thoughts occupy your mind? When you are faced with a difficult task, how do you describe yourself and your chances of success? When you are despised and rejected by others, what do you say to yourself? When you have just fallen below the standards of God, what do you say to you? How do you describe you when you have just failed?

It has been said again and again there is a world of difference between half-full and half-empty in describing a glass of water. The former tells you, you are close to filling up the glass; the latter gives you a perception you have just begun. One inspires you to go ahead and complete what you have started; the other builds in you an inertia that is hard to break.

Leaders need to be careful the way they describe themselves. Pulling yourself down may seem convenient and logical but it offers no benefit. Being positive is not being untruthful. It is recognizing another truth different from the one presenting itself. In any situation, there are at least two truths – the truth of your present situation and the truth of God's view on it. Speaking God's truth to yourself is often not convenient and logical, but it may be the only way you preserve yourself for real living and especially for effective communication. Do yourself a favour; speak positive words to yourself.

- ### *Positive and enthusiastic attitude to life*

When last did you wake up in the morning and punch the air, saying to yourself: This is the day that the Lord has made; I shall rejoice and be glad in it? Most people will prefer to allow the circumstances to determine their moods. Effective communicators choose to do otherwise. Through effective self-talk, they order the circumstances around them. They look at the positive side of life and see life unfolding beautifully for them. Their confidence is infectious – affecting every of their endeavours, especially communication.

You may ask; what has enthusiasm got to do with it? A lot, I must say. It is not easy to dismiss an enthusiastic man. Enthusiasm is not at variance with sobriety, with which we are advised to carry on in the world. To be sure, enthusiasm derives its root from the Greek word, *Ethos*, meaning "in God". Enthusiasm is a divine attribute. Only few attributes prepare you better for interpersonal communication than enthusiasm.

Self-talk is needed during preparation as well as during delivery. Effective communicators always spend time talking to themselves before delivering their speeches. They rehearse their speeches, work on their gestures, anticipate responses, try out several punch lines, and select appropriate humour…all in their minds. This mental preparation almost invariably leads to effective communication.

SELF IMAGE – SELF TALK – SPEECH CYCLE

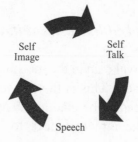

Self Image   Self Talk

Speech   *Figure 2*

What Has Self-Image Got To Do With It?

If self-image is the way we perceive ourselves, then it is responsible for the way we talk to ourselves. Our self-talk is a projection of who we think we are. The emphasis is on who we think we are rather than who we really are. We promote what we value; rewarding it with thoughts that advance the value we place on it.

The experience of the spies that went to Jericho speaks volumes to their generation as well as to ours. Ten of the twelve spies saw themselves as grasshoppers. Before they came up with their damning report, saying, *"We can't attack those people; they are stronger than we are,"* they had already said in their hearts, *"We seemed like grasshoppers in our own eyes, and we looked the same to them."* [Numbers 13:31-33]

Their self-talk supported the value they placed on themselves. It was not long before they spoke and acted in ways that corroborated their self-image as well as the resulting self-talk.

Is this all about thinking positively about ourselves? That is only if positively means aligning ourselves with the will of God for our lives. When we assume a grandiose view of us not supported by the Scriptures, it only breeds arrogance and self-deceit.

> *"Do not think of yourself more highly than you ought, but rather think of yourself with sober judgment, in accordance with the faith God has*

distributed to each of you." Romans 12:3
"Let this mind be in you, which was also in
Christ Jesus:" Philippians 2:5

The closer we are to seeing ourselves the way God sees us, the better self-image we have. Only a self-image that is aligned with God produces a self-talk that powers our speeches and guarantees impact on the lives of our listeners.

CHAPTER

05

ARE YOU IMPULSIVE?

It was not the best of times for Hannah. Years of barrenness had increased her agony. She was first of two wives and the eye of Elkanah, her husband. But all of these Hannah would readily trade off for just one child. Peninnah – her mate – had sons for their husband and did everything possible to remind Hannah of her barrenness. The Bible records, "Peninnah, her rival, would torment and humiliate her…This went on year after year; whenever they went to the house of the LORD, Peninnah would upset Hannah so much that she would cry and refuse to eat anything. With a rival like Peninnah, there was no respite for Hannah.

In one of such annual trips to the house of the Lord, Hannah decided she had to take her case to the Lord. She refused food but welcomed tears despite entreaties from her caring husband. In her distress, she cried bitterly to the Lord. She made a passionate appeal to God to consider her situation.

Her head was buried in her hands, her eyes swollen from protracted weeping. When you are agonizing in prayers, you have no time to think of custom and tradition. She never bothered to find out if she was verbalizing her agony. Her concern was getting across to the One who could help her. And she thought she was getting through. Until someone strolled into the temple.

Eli was the High Priest. He was the custodian of God's law. He stopped abruptly at the sight of Hannah. Not that it was strange to see a woman in the temple. There was something else Eli noticed that was strange and condemnable. Hannah's lips were moving but no words were coming out of them. The last time Eli saw that, the person was drunk and luckily it was not in the temple. The Bible records:

> *"As she kept on praying to the LORD, Eli observed her mouth. Hannah was praying in her heart, and her lips were moving but her voice was not heard. Eli thought she was drunk and said to her, "How long will you keep on getting drunk? Get rid of your wine." I Samuel 1:12-14*

Eli observed, thought and spoke. His observation was right - Hannah's mouth was moving but her voice was not heard. We cannot prevent ourselves from observing. Our five senses are there to pick signals from our environment. We see, we feel, we hear, we taste and we smell. These senses keep us alive. We will be dead without them. We run away from fire to safety because our senses pick up danger signals. We run to the waiting arms of a loving spouse because we sense a welcome in their voices, faces or actions. Our senses keep us alive.

As Christians, our senses keep us in constant contact with God's world. As his ambassadors and agents of change, our senses inform us of the happenings in the main theatre of God's creation. We watch over the world for God through our senses.

Eli must have felt like one of us. After all, he was God's ordained High Priest; a true descendant of Levi and one of the last judges of God's people. On this particular day, his senses were at alert. It was the period of the annual pilgrimage and Jews had come from all over the world to Jerusalem to worship. Think of this period like the time of a major Christian festival. May be, an International Christian conference that draws worshippers from many nations of the world. Eli was the chief host and expectedly at his spiritual best. His senses were at attention to sight any infringement of God's holy laws.

He had just noticed something unusual – in God's house!

Next to observing, Eli thought. Eli's senses sent signals to his mind. His mind took up the challenge. It decoded the message as rapidly as it got it. There was no reason to ponder for a long time. His might not be a jet-age like ours, but there were many patrons of the Temple at this time of the year to spend so much time dwelling on one case. Eli's mind looked out for a short cut. Like a computer, it looked for installed software – programmed to process input in a predetermined pattern. This readily available software is that of feeling and experience. Eli's mind quickly recalled a similar experience. The answer came out almost instantly, screaming – She is drunk! She is drunk! She is drunk!

Eli quickly picked up the printout and like a manager working to beat a deadline, acted on the report without the benefit of crosschecking.

> He spoke. *"How long are you going to stay drunk? Put away your wine."* 1 Samuel 1:14

Eli spoke on impulse. He depended too heavily on his experience. He ignited his vocal chord without thinking. He had been assured by his experience that what he saw was right. In fact, he was persuaded his conclusion was infallible, the only truth there was. That force that propelled him on to speak without checking is called *Initial Reaction.* It is a force we must all admit is strong. It is like love at first sight, only stronger. It suspends our sense of reasoning and turns us into slaves of our experiences. We become like machines running predictable schedules. We become like animals responding to external stimuli in predictable fashion.

He was wrong. We are usually wrong when we move swiftly from observation to speech without the benefit of deep thinking. Hasty judgment of people and events may seem convenient, but it least prepares us for an effective Christian witness. Let's consider some of the hasty judgments we make regarding some of the observations made above.

What would you think of a lady in a skimpy dress in a church where you are a leader? What runs through your mind when in the course of ministry activity, you see a guy whose eyes dash everywhere where the girls are seated while the prayer is going on? You have just seen a woman with a sad face backing a child and pulling two others as she finds her way to your church's organized crusade. What immediately comes to your mind? You are about to put out the light in your home and bid the night a farewell when you hear noise in your neighbour's home. Through your half-opened window you see your neighbour staggers to his door and fumbles with the key. What conclusion do you reach? You are a student and a Christian. Your classmate has been late in doing his assignments in the past, claiming she had gone to night party. Today, she has failed to submit her assignment again. What do you think is responsible for her failure to keep the assignment submission deadline? You are a professional sharing an office with a number of colleagues. One of them is reputed for using vulgar language. An argument arises in the office and this colleague is about to give his opinion. What are the chances that you will prevent him from making a contribution if you were the moderator?

If you have answered the above questions with reliance on your feeling and past experience, you are not alone. Most people operate in what is called the reactionary mode, where they respond to people and events based on the initial reaction. The initial reaction is a product of our feelings and experience. In this reactionary mode, the communicator is not always assured of the best response, as reliance on experience can sometimes be arbitrary and inconclusive. Christian witnesses who operate in this mode are not in any way better than programmed machines. They are slaves to their feeling and experience and respond to people and issues in a predetermined manner. They are judgmental. They capitalize on their differences with the non-Christian rather than their commonalities. They drive the listeners away from them and from their message. The listener is often forced to reply in kind, attacking the speaker to protect his territory and stalling the communication process.

As people are not always predicable like machines, the reactionary response does not provide the basis for an effective communication. Like Eli, reactive communicators are often wrong.

We succumb to the power of the Initial Reaction because it is natural to do so. It makes the first call ahead of reason. It appears without invitation. It stands there, staring you in the face and daring you to think. But you, my reader, did not get to where you are today by always doing the natural. You didn't so much like school but you persuaded yourself to go through it. The natural instinct is to eat all you can wherever and whenever you can. Many health issues after, we are learning to endure some of the foods that are not sweet to the taste but necessary for the body. In both cases, what we have done was to challenge our former experiences and cultivate new ones that ensure we lead quality lives. We dared the power of the Initial Reaction and refused to fall for its lies.

In communication, the initial reaction holds sway. It governs most of our communication. And it does so with reckless abandon because we are lazy. Strenuous thinking seems to be too much work to fit into our busy schedules. So, we fall into the trap of looking for a template that fits into our instant action style. And feelings and experience come in handy. Initial reaction is the voice of our feelings and of our experiences. So, we speak on impulse. This kind of communication is called Reactive Communication. It's our passport to destroying the world. Unleashed upon a marriage, this style of communication destroys trust and makes mutual coexistence a nightmare. Replicated in a Christian ministry, it reduces the leader's level of impact. It is the reason why your personal relationships are what they are today. And it would determine how far you go in living a life of impact.

Can there be situations where Reactive Communication will make sense? Yes, on very few occasions that bother on life and death. I don't have to analyze fire before I run away from it. With a mob of attackers approaching my way, instant conversation with my legs makes sense. Pulling my child out of danger is another example. I believe you can add more. But I am sure you can't fill the page with such situations because they are few. In most cases, our best bet is to question the Initial Reaction to examine its appropriateness to the situation at hand. It is the least we can do to impact our listeners.

Got The Guts?

Leaders who challenge the initial reaction get guts. It's not natural to do so. It's like swimming against the tide. They choose the rational over the irrational. They dare to dispute the seemingly unassailable fact, as presented by their feelings and experiences. They choose proactive communication over reactive communication. In the process, they take responsibility for their responses instead of handling the responsibility to the Initial Reaction.

To be sure, proactive communicators do not underestimate the power of the Initial Reaction. They recognize both its passion and ferocity. They know it's a moving train you can't easily stop. And it's their understanding of initial reaction and its dire consequences that motivates them to challenge its claims. They know that the initial reaction might end up being the right response to the situation. But they want to be sure. They are not comfortable giving over their power of choice to their feelings and experiences. They have chosen to take charge under God.

And so, they create alternative responses to the one being suggested by the Initial Reaction. They stop to think. Is this the most appropriate response? Are there other responses they can adopt? Stopping to think dampens the power of the initial reaction. Its seeming arrogance wears off the moment proactive communicators stop to think. They no longer see from the parochial prism of Initial Reaction. They have been freed up to create alternative responses. Armed with alternative responses, they proceed to take the best course of action – the most appropriate response that is in sync with their Christian values. It is after then that they respond. They are satisfied with going through this process again and again even if they end up affirming the initial reaction. They are happy to have taken charge of their response. If my reader has never experienced the feeling of this freedom, it might be worth it to give it a try. It should be obvious that proactive communication results from an effective self-talk. With this self-talk they are empowered to respond proactively instead of reactively. Proactivity is therefore the power to choose our response.

Hypothetically, put yourself in Hannah's shoes. How would you have responded to Eli's verbal abuse? Before you respond, let me give you some background story. You are Hannah, a respectable woman. You are the first wife of Elkanah, arguably a rich man from the tribe of Ephraim. Your gifts and offerings keep the priests and their families alive. You have everything going on for you, including the love of your husband, except a child. Now, you have just been insulted.

Wouldn't you have blown your top? Wouldn't you have asked a pertinent question just as a friendly reminder? Like: "Do you know who you have just insulted? Do I look like one of those ordinary Jews that you could insult anyhow?" You probably would have walked away, hissing and cursing, "Anyway, it is not your fault".

That is what most victims of reactionary communication do - they respond in kind. But Hannah was cast in a different mould. She chose a well-reasoned response.

"Not so, my lord," Hannah replied, "I am a woman who is deeply troubled. I have not been drinking wine or beer; I was pouring out my soul

> *to the LORD. Do not take your servant for a*
> *wicked woman; I have been praying here out of*
> *my great anguish and grief." I Samuel. 1:15, 16*

Hannah had the option to operate in the reactive mode. She had alternatives but she decided the best response. In essence, Hannah acknowledged the power of the initial reaction but chose to respond based on a choice from a number of alternatives. Hannah was proactive.

Proactivity is the power to choose our response.

Figure 3

Proactive communicators take a moment to reflect on what they observe before they speak. That moment of reflection can produce insight, which gives power to their speech. That was Nehemiah's experience when he took a moment before answering the King on his plan to rebuild the wall. That was the experience of David at Ziklag, when he 'encouraged himself in the Lord' before he spoke in the time of distress.

IMPULSE - CONSIDERATION - SPEECH DYNAMICS

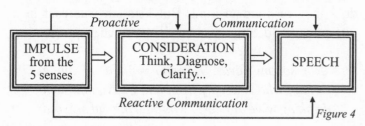

Figure 4

CHAPTER

06

ARE YOU RISK-AVERSE?

A friend once told me why he would not want to give Jesus the control of his life. He feared that the deepening relationship with Jesus would expose his sins and he might be forced to make certain changes that he would not like to make, at least not until he was seventy. Another told me years after he had become a Christian how he used to run away from me because I reminded him of his inadequacies and feared he might be forced to own up to me that he needed help.

Even as Christians, we fear going the whole hog with God as he might ask us to do something stupid, like selling all we have and moving to Iraq as a missionary. I have heard someone said, "If you climb up too close to God, he might shake the tree."

If we are so suspicious of the God we cannot see, we are more suspicious of our fellow men. We run away from deep and affectionate relationship that leaves us vulnerable. We hate being hurt; so we stay away. We hate ridicule; so we cover up our shortcomings.

We started covering up early. Adam and Eve had an excellent relationship with God and with each other until disobedience crept in. Suddenly, they found themselves naked. It was the height of vulnerability. And they did what humanity has been doing ever since; they looked for a physical covering and went into hiding. As we hide from each other and from God, our relationships have become superficial, lacking the depth needed to bring healing and growth. We have become masquerades, adorning masks that cover our inadequacies and projecting who we want to be rather than who we really are. We think that takes us from the dangerous and shifty ground of risk and pitches us on the safe and stable ground of peace.

We are dead wrong. Openness or transparency may be risky, but it is the only way to develop deep and beneficial relationships with God and with each other. It is the only way we can build others up and impact our world.

> *"Whoever conceals their sins does not prosper,*
> *but the one who confesses and renounces them*
> *finds mercy." Proverbs 28: 13*

Until we remove our masks and own up to our shortcomings, we cannot expect a cordial relationship with God. Our prosperity lies not in the safety of a life behind the mask but in the adventurous and risky life of telling God as it is. We can learn a lot about the way David and Saul reacted to their sin. Saul wanted a cover up so he could have a favourable perception from the people. He lost. David, after being confronted with his sin, owned up and repented. He won.

God also demands openness before each other.

> *"Therefore confess your sins to each other and pray for each other so that you may be healed. The prayer of a righteous person is powerful and effective." James 5:16*

Our healing – personal and relational – is found in openness and not in masquerading. Our relationships almost invariably move to a new level, when the level of our openness increases.

Playing The Masquerades

We all play the masquerades to varying degrees, especially when it comes to communication. We tend to masquerade more in communication than in any other activity. In masquerading, we take on a part that is not real – a part that insulates us from whom we really are and confers on us an undue advantage. Have you practiced silence when you knew speaking would mean owning up to your guilt? I did a lot of that as a kid. On normal days, as a child, I was outspoken – sometimes boisterous – ever eager to air my views on a variety of issues. But I usually played the dumb anytime mom asked who messed the floor or who was responsible for a missing piece of meat in the kitchen. It never worked with my mom. She almost always found out I was the culprit. When she did, the charges against me would go up by two – obstruction of justice and wastage of mama's valuable time. The punishment, of course, increased with the charges.

I hate to admit that I still play the dumb sometimes. When on the plane and I get a notch to share the gospel with the guy on the next seat, I weigh my options. If the guy has pulled out a pornographic magazine or said an obscene word against the gospel in the course of the flight, I tend to pretend to be sleeping. I see attack on my values coming if I open up a conversation around Jesus that might make me look stupid. I play safe. So, mum's the word. It still takes a great deal of effort to brake from that inertia and venture out on the risky terrain of opening up that I am a Christian and that I would like to discuss about my faith. Where I have broken the culture of silence and opened myself to probable ridicule, the effort has been worth it. I have seen men and women that looked impossible to reach succumbing to the gospel – 'the power of God unto salvation". I have seen it so many times that I am emboldened to think, 'the harder they come; the easier they fall'. I must admit, that has only made it a little easier. I still have my trepidation.

Levels of Communication

Our level of safety consciousness or risk aversion will determine how effective we will be as Christian witnesses. The most risk averse among Christians operates strictly on the Cliché level. This is a safe haven. It is the domain of superficial communication. It is the terrain of *Jesus loves you, God bless you, I am praying for you*... Statements that have lost their meaning because of abuse and carry no power to bring change to the hearers. This is where you locate the hapless smile you give to your neighbour and the regular but non-committal *How are you?* you haul at your office colleague. It is the unfancied *I love you* you say to a motherless baby on your church visit to the home. It rears its ugly head as you throw a coin at the beggar or homeless on the street during traffic; and as you bundle gospel tracts at the reception of a bank while you look around to be sure no one is watching.

ENCOUNTER LEVEL: Absolute openness and honesty exposing personal and emotional state of the communicator.

FEELING LEVEL: Here, the communicator involves himself intellectually and emotionally. He is true to his emotional feeling

JUDGEMENT LEVEL: The communicator states his ideas and judgments but cautious of negative response. [Matt 19:16-22]

FACT LEVEL: Gossip level. The communicator does not share anything personal.

CLICHÉ LEVEL. Superficial communication. No sharing involved. Mere statements without meaning

Levels of Interpersonal Communication

In each of these cases, you are in charge, calling the shots and determining the communication boundaries. On this level, you retain your space, your comfort zone. You don't have to reveal your struggles. You don't have to discuss your recalcitrant children. They also don't bother you with their problems. To allow them to do so is to saddle you with their responsibilities. Given that you already have a lot on your plate, this is an invasion of your privacy and of your space. Your instincts scream endlessly, *Defend your space, Guard your territory.* Beyond your set of white teeth (assuming you have one), the non-Christian sees nothing and knows nothing. That seems pretty safe; doesn't it?

Most often, the Christians play Peter – boisterous in the Church and tongue-tied in the public. Peter had a reputation of asking the toughest questions. He stood up when others were comfortable being seated. He was not a man to shy away from controversy. He wanted Jesus to scuttle his plan and stay forever on the Mountain of Transfiguration. He even rebuked Jesus when he insisted he would go to the Cross. But he did all of these in his comfort zone, in the company of Jesus and other disciples. Once when he was out of his comfort zone, Peter lost his voice. He settled for passivity. He chose the usual culture of silence. He did this not once but thrice. He denied Christ. His cliché was "I never knew him'. And he said that while it mattered most. He said it where a bold stand would have brought credibility to the claim of Jesus. But in saying it, he saved his neck. That is the goal of cliché communication. It absolves us of responsibility and saves us from ridicule. But then, it takes the claim of Jesus out of the public square, restricts it to the four walls of the church, and prevents the spread of the enduring culture that is capable of transforming the society.

Besides, Jesus said, *"But whoever disowns me before others, I will disown before my Father in heaven."* *[Matthew 10:33]* Cliché communication helps us shy away from getting involved in other people's lives and makes us less vulnerable. But it also leads to the loss of a relationship that is most vital to our lives. Jesus' denial of us is by far a greater loss than our comfort and safety.

So, the choice is between cliché and commitment, between stagnation and personal growth, between convenience and responsibility, and between personal safety and societal decline.

But why do most Christians choose to communicate at the cliché level despite the obvious disadvantage to their personal survival and the expansion of the kingdom of God? The love of convenience is attractive. The temptation to stay away from the challenges of relating to people at a deeper level is real. Only the well-motivated Christians break from the power of this love. Only those who wish to be like Jesus resist this temptation.

Some Christians go beyond the Cliché level to a slightly higher level – Fact or Gossip level. Here, the Christian is smart. He sees the need to communicate the gospel and tries to break the inertia of reaching out to the lost world. But he minimizes his risks by limiting himself to issues that reveal nothing about himself. He detaches himself from the message. He says, 'Listen to what I have to say, but don't bother me or about me'. This includes communicating other people's message without having thought deeply about them. Or quoting a scripture that yet to make an impact in our lives. It also includes the gossip you share without having corroborated it. This communication is cold and lacks the power to build up the listener. Essentially, to the Christians who operate on this level, the gospel is not something to which they are experientially involved with. It is a gospel they identify with intellectually. It is what they heard, not what they have. It is gossip, not truth. But Jesus said, *"Then you will know the truth, and the truth will set you free." [John 8:32]* This type of communication stands little chance of changing lives.

Picture the rich young ruler in Matthew 19. In our days, he would be an interviewer's delight. He was very forthcoming with answers. He had just the right mixture of intelligence and impressive personality. He was rich. He was young. I guess he was also handsome. Money makes the difference, you know. His encounter with Jesus revealed another plus for this extraordinary young man – he was ready to learn. At least, so it seemed. He asked Jesus hard questions and listened to his answers. He responded to Jesus' questions with equal candour.

Then…

Then, Jesus touched a sore point. The young man took offense. He became very cautious. His openness became suspect. He withdrew to his shell. The turf had become tough. He wanted out. He stepped back. He left sorrowful.

The rich young ruler operated at the Judgment level. He

went beyond the Fact or Gossip level. He stepped beyond the intellectual plane. He stepped on the emotional plane. But he had one leg on the plane, just in case. He was cautious of negative response. He took negative response personally. When the going got tough, it was easy for him to go back to his shell.

There are Christians who operate on this level in their relationships with non-Christians. They step out to reach the hurting world but are cautious of negative response to their witness. Supposing they ask questions that I can't answer? Supposing they discover I still have issues I am dealing with? This hesitation could be out of experience or out of fear or both. But it is there, sounding a cautionary alarm and restricting the witness' openness and eroding his confidence.

I remember my encounter with some Christian students as a Moslem in my student days. An argument had developed in their attempt to reach me with the gospel. Their initial enthusiasm began to wane as I took up difficult issues with them. I tried to discredit the Bible as the Word of God. I challenged the deity of Jesus. Trinity, I asserted, was the figment of their polytheistic imaginations. Then, I wanted to know why Mary and Martha were competing for Jesus' attention. When they were not immediately forthcoming with an answer, I shared my preconceived conclusion. Jesus was seeing both of them; you know, in an amorous way. That did it. They flared up. They just could not take it.

Like the rich young ruler, they took offense. They stepped back. They walked away. And as they walked away, they did the unfathomable. They started to curse me. They said that I had blasphemed the name of the Lord and deserved judgement. It was a drama of the absurd and the losers were the Judgment level communicators. As for me, I relished watching them angry. I celebrated my victory, but not for long.

Christian witnesses who operate at the Feeling level are intellectually and emotionally involved in their communication efforts with non-Christians. They are ever willing to share their lives with others. This adventurous life has its challenges, but the alternative is far worse. Communicating with the world at a deeper level helps us reach it effectively. The world will not let down its guard until we have let down ours. The non-Christian will wear his mask as long as we wear ours. As we become more vulnerable in speech and relationship building, we are able to descend from the judgment seat and touch the lives of people for whom Jesus died.

Once Mopelola and I had a misunderstanding, as we sometimes do. We threw caution to the wind and started shouting at each other. In the middle of the fight, there was a knock on the door. Immediately, we put on our masquerade's costumes. Within seconds, we started acting the perfect couple as our non-Christian friend walked in. As he sat down to a glass of water, I decided to stop the drama and own up that we have just had a quarrel. I then asked our friend to pray for us. The shock on his face spoke volumes. After a minute of staring at me, he spoke out. "You mean you two also quarrel?" My response was swift, "Who do you think we are – angels? We quarrel, sometimes, big time. Especially when we take our eyes away from God and concentrate on our egos. But God has a way of helping us pull together again, as we reconnect with him and through him with each other." My friend didn't feel comfortable praying for us. But I nudged him on until he did. He went like, "Lord, you know Mope and Abiodun are good people. It's the devil that's trying to destroy their joy. Please don't let him succeed." Two weeks after, my friend became a Christian.

By far the deepest level of communication we can operate from with the world is the Encounter level. This is a state of absolute openness and honesty exposing personal and emotional state of the communicator. This is what Jesus did when he took on the form of man. He put himself in our shoes in order to communicate with us at the deepest level. He was tempted just like we are. He hungered. He thirsted. He was betrayed. He felt affection. He paid taxes. He ate. He had a childhood. Jesus lived in a real world, a world he graciously and deeply shared with sinners. He was at the tax offices, reputed for their corruption. He went to dinner with notorious people. He just did not seem to have enough of controversially courting sinners. They were the reason why he came; the reason why he lived, the purpose for which he died, and the hope for which he rose from the dead.

Someone I know closely was caught in adulterous relationship that almost destroyed his life, home and ministry. Most of his close friends ran away, not wanting to be tainted by his sin. He became a pariah of some sort. But one stayed. He flew to his city, despite protestations from other friends. In an emotionally charged meeting, he listened with rapt attention to the story of a fallen brother.

In minutes, both were in tears. They were just crying before the Lord. There were no accusations. No lectures. Then, they prayed. They cried some more. And then, they prayed. The fallen brother has since gotten back on his feet. When asked why he sought his fallen brother out, he said, *"Let any one of you who is without sin be the first to throw a stone." [John 8:7]*

That was an encounter level communication.

Jesus Has Shown The Way

Jesus communicated at the deepest level with man. He opened himself to wide that we spat on, accused him wrongly, whipped him, tossed him around like a common criminal, crowned him with thorns and nailed him on the cross. He abandoned all for us – his divinity, his rights, and his priviledges – to level with us.

> *"Think of yourselves the way Christ Jesus thought of himself. He had equal status with God but didn't think so much of himself that he had to cling to the advantages of that status no matter what. Not at all. When the time came, he set aside the privileges of deity and took on the status of a slave, became human! Having become human, he stayed human. It was an incredibly humbling process. He didn't claim special privileges. Instead, he lived a selfless, obedient life and then died a selfless, obedient death—and the worst kind of death at that—a crucifixion." Philippians 2:5-8 [MSG]*

Then, he took our place before his father. He became sin and got punished for us big time – in order to fulfill the ransom placed on our heads.

"He God made him who had no sin to be sin for us, so that in him we might become the righteousness of God." 2 Corinthians 5:21

Alleluia! He rose from the dead! He is now seated at the right hand of God. And you think he is done with us? No way. His identification with us is beyond comprehension. Let me allow the scriptures to speak for itself.

"It wasn't so long ago that you were mired in that old stagnant life of sin. You let the world, which doesn't know the first thing about living, tell you how to live. You filled your lungs with polluted unbelief, and then exhaled disobedience. We all did it, all of us doing what we felt like doing, when we felt like doing it, all of us in the same boat. It's a wonder God didn't lose his temper and do away with the whole lot of us. Instead, immense in mercy and with an incredible love, he embraced us. He took our sin-dead lives and made us alive in Christ. He did all this on his own, with no help from us! Then he picked us up and set us down in highest heaven in company with Jesus, our Messiah." Philippians 2:1-4 [MSG]

He expects us to do the same for our fellow men. And Paul has given us the blueprints on how to do just that.

"Even though I am free of the demands and expectations of everyone, I have voluntarily become a servant to any and all in order to reach a wide range of people: religious, nonreligious, meticulous moralists, loose-living immoralists, the defeated, the demoralized—whoever. I didn't take on their way of life. I kept my bearings in Christ—but I entered their world and tried to experience things from their point of view. I've become just about every sort of servant there is in my attempts to lead those I meet into a God-saved life. I did all this because of the Message. I didn't just want to talk about it; I wanted to be in on it!" 1 Corinthians 9:19-23 [MSG]

Are You Risk-Averse?

True and effective communication is a risky business. We must be intellectually and emotionally involved with the non-Christians and with our fellowmen, if we desire to build them up and impact them. Obviously, it is not every communication that should be at the deepest level. A meeting with a stranger at the store might be better to end up with a delightful and heartfelt, "It was nice meeting you," Or, "Have a nice day and God bless you." Saying those words and meaning them takes them beyond the cliché level and ensures impact. Sometimes, it might be expeditious to walk away from an argument, without mounting a defense. And you do not have to share your deepest secret at every drop of the hat. And there are some secrets that are better confessed to the Lord than to man. But as much as the opportunity presents itself and the

Spirit leads us, we must stay the course, communicating intellectually and emotionally with the world.

The benefit far outweighs the risk.

07

A PROCESS, NOT AN EVENT

Have you ever driven a car? Yes? Then, you understand what a process is. You can easily identify the interacting elements in a driving process. You, the driver, are an element interacting with other elements like the car, the other road users, the law enforcement agents, the road and the traffic lights or signs. Each of these elements is vital to effective and safe driving. If your car is good and the road is bad, your life and the car are at risk unless other elements make necessary adjustments to accommodate the deficiency. Like, you slowing down in response to a road sign that warns you of the bad surface ~a hundred yards ahead.

If another driver leaves his lane and faces you, setting up a head-on collision, what do the other elements in the driving process do? You got it. They adjust to meet the new challenges posed by an interacting element. You may blast your horn and the car driver hopefully moves to his lane, in response to your alert. You may swerve the car to safety. Or, a traffic officer around can intervene to save the situation. The goal is to restore sanity and keep driving safe.

Like driving, communication is a process. There are a variety of interacting elements in the communication process. They include:

- The speaker, source, sender or communicator
- The message
- The listener, the receiver or the audience
- The medium

THE COMMUNICATION PROCESS

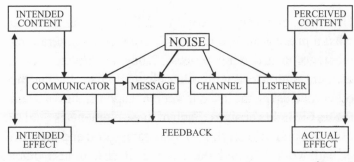

Figure 5

The figure shows the communication process. The process starts with you, the Christian witness as the communicator, the speaker or the initiator conceiving an idea (or intended content) that you wish to pass across to a non-Christian listener with an intended effect. Your intention may be to challenge him to consider reading the

Bible as a source of guidance for successful living.

So, you package this content into a message. The central theme of your message is to make your listener consider and possibly decide to make the Bible the source of his guidance in life. That is your message. What channel you choose to get your message across depends on a number of factors. You may wish to write it on a note and pass it across to him. The written message could be a poem or prose. It could be a drama. You don't have to be the author of the message. You may be passing across a book on the topic. Hopefully, it is a book you have read and consider relevant to the listener's need. You might want to package your message into words. If you choose the latter, which is the most frequent, your channel is speech.

Let us assume you have decided to present your message as a speech. You have your idea, you have your message and you have chosen your channel. You are ready to deliver it to the listener. The listener is also called the receiver or the audience.

Now, as the figure indicates, the man standing before you is not a dummy. He has a thinking faculty and has his own perceptions about life and other issues. If you have not considered all these in your intended content, the choice of your channel and the packaging of your message, you might receive a rude shock. For example, you might be witnessing to a preacher of many years, just because you have not bothered to find out first. You might be speaking to a deaf man, because you have been more concerned about your message than the recipient. You might discover the man you are about to speak English to speaks only Spanish. If, on the other hand, you have thoroughly considered the listener, you might be able to save the day. Whatever the case, the listener has a perception of your message, called the perceived content. His perceptions have coloured the message. He might think you are a representative of a Bible publisher. He might think you are out of touch with reality and needs to have your head examined. He might wonder why someone had never told him this before now. He might say, "I sure want to know more about this book". His perception of what constitutes the message represents the actual effect.

You may say, "Try the Bible, it is the best source of guidance for a successful living." The listener may hear, "Buy the Bible, it the best way to become a successful Bible publisher representative like me."

Oops! You can imagine the distortion of the original intent. The deviation between the intended effect and the actual effect is wide. An inexperienced witness can be alarmed by this deviation and may think the non-Christian is pulling a fast one on him. This may be true in some cases. Experienced witness sees this as an opportunity to employ feedback to clarify issues and reduce the variation between the intended content and the actual effect. With the reduction of the distortion, the two may come close to having the same understanding about the issue. The listener then has the opportunity to make a decision based on a well-communicated message.

But there are other forces the speaker has to contend with – the noise that seeks to drown his voice and his message. A noise is defined as anything that interferes between the speaker and the listener that is capable of distorting the communication process. It's also called interference. Noise constitutes barriers to effective communication. And, as you must have observed, it affects all the interacting elements in the communication process.

Drowned Voices

Try and preach the gospel to a woman in a noisy African market or at a busy train station during rush hour in the West. Your voice will hardly be distinguishable from the noise of price haggling and the whistles of trains. The noise here is environmental and is capable of altering your message. It includes noise from transport, industrial or recreational activities. The noise could also be physical as in someone talking near the listener or a distraction from a crying baby or someone else seeking the listener's attention. It could be semantic as in the speaker using a word of phrase that is not clear or that conveys a different meaning to the listener. For example, you may say, "Accept Jesus as Lord over your life" and the listener, who has suffered from the hands of brutal leaders, may hear, "Accept Jesus as a dictator".

The noise could also be spiritual.

> *"They traveled through the whole island until they came to Paphos. There they met a Jewish sorcerer and false prophet named Bar-Jesus, who was an attendant of the proconsul, Sergius Paulus. The proconsul, an intelligent man, sent for Barnabas and Saul because he wanted to hear the word of God. But Elymas the sorcerer*

(for that is what his name means) opposed them and tried to turn the proconsul from the faith. Then Saul, who was also called Paul, filled with the Holy Spirit, looked straight at Elymas and said, "You are a child of the devil and an enemy of everything that is right! You are full of all kinds of deceit and trickery. Will you never stop perverting the right ways of the Lord? Now the hand of the Lord is against you. You are going to be blind, and for a time you will be unable to see the light of the sun." Immediately mist and darkness came over him, and he groped about, seeking someone to lead him by the hand." Acts 13:6-11

As soon as the spiritual noise was overcome, the message got through.

"When the proconsul saw what had happened, he believed, for he was amazed at the teaching about the Lord." Acts 13:12

Paul said, *"And even if our gospel is veiled, it is veiled to those who are perishing. The god of this age has blinded the minds of unbelievers, so that they cannot see the light of the gospel of the glory of Christ, who is the image of God." 2 Corinthians 4: 3-4*

Sin, of any kind, is a type of spiritual noise.

An effective witness must be well prayed up and filled with the Holy Spirit like Paul to wield the spiritual authority needed to overcome spiritual noise. The deliverance of the souls of men is a spiritual warfare and only the spiritually violent takes it by the force of the Spirit.

The noise may be attitudinal. The woman at the well in John 4 experienced an attitudinal noise - Samaritans had no dealings with the Jews. It may be economical. The economic state of a woman stands between her and a Christian witness and may prevent the gospel from reaching her in the form intended. The noise may also be emotional. A disturbed mind is a stumbling block to an effective witness if not discovered by the witness. It may be psychological as in hunger or tiredness.

Once a speaker recognizes the noise, it is important to address the issue concerned, rather than gloss over it. The noise often grows louder with neglect. Any speaker that fails to give the noise the attention it needs has contributed to the failure of the communication process. Jesus fed the multitudes to address a noise. He engaged the Samaritan woman at the well to address a noise. Paul prayed for and raised Euticus from the dead to address a noise. Just as he did in the case of the proconsul. Indeed, most miracles are God's ways of removing the barriers to the effective communication of his truth to mankind. In most of these cases, the noise may be the launching pad for the witness to build a case for the gospel and ensure an effective witness.

There is a lot more you need to know about an effective Christian witness.

08

DARE TO BE A WITNESS

Do you want a lifetime advice? Be a Christian witness. And if you can take one more advice, here it is – Be the very best witness you can be.

There are a thousand and one reasons why you would not want to stick your neck out for your faith and strike that conversation with a non-Christian. It is a tough call, I know. Speaking in public is one of humanity's greatest fears. Some say, it places first ahead of fear of death and fear of snakes. So, you are not being strange when you hold your tongue before a needy friend or perspire in your sweat when compelled to stand and defend your faith before a crowd.

But for every reason you want out of witnessing, there is a

more compelling reason why you should witness. The reason is you. The real you will not let you keep quiet when the occasion demands that you take a stand. The real you will break the inertia and initiate that conversation. The real you will break the culture of silence and passivity. That is, if you know the real you.

Most Christians live with little knowledge of who they are. It is a tragedy of monumental proportion. It is as tragic as a salesman that goes out on a sales campaign and forgets who he is, his brief, his assets, his products and the company he represents.

There are certainly many more, but two pairs of metaphors describe you. If these were my idea, you could debate it. But they are what the Scriptures say about you. If you doubt this, you could as well doubt your existence. Will you dare to look in the mirror of God and see who you really are? If we are looking at the same mirror, here is what you will see:

- You are the light of the world and the salt of the earth.
- You are a priest and a king.

> "You are the salt of the earth. But if the salt loses its saltiness, how can it be made salty again? It is no longer good for anything, except to be thrown out and trampled by men. "You are the light of the world. A town built on a hill cannot be hidden. Neither do people light a lamp and put it under a bowl. Instead they put it on its stand, and it gives light to everyone in the house. In the same way, let your light shine before

others, that they may see your good deeds and glorify your Father in heaven." Matthew 5:13-16

"And hath made us kings and priests to His God and Father; to him be glory and dominion forever and ever. Amen." Revelation 1:6 [NKJV]

Are you a woman or a man? Do you have a problem being a man or a woman? I doubt very much. It is what you have been made to be. It is not the environment that determines your gender; God did. You only have challenges when you as a man decide to take on the nature of a woman. Then, you shouldn't have any problem with relating to your nature as light and salt. The only problem is you did not start out being light and salt like you did in being a woman or a man. Your New Birth experience conferred that new nature on you. Well, it does not matter at all whether it is a biological nature or a spiritual nature. Nature is "the inherent character or basic constitution of a person or thing" or "an inner force or the sum of such forces in an individual".

It is your inherent character to be the light; your basic constitution is salt. That is why you experience an inner force to shine as light to show the way to your hurting world. That is why you experience an inner compulsion to sweeten, preserve and purify your society. It is probably because of this inner force that you are reading this book. If you don't feel this inner tugging, something is wrong. And you should be concerned. The same way you should be concerned if as a man or woman you do not have the natural instincts associated with a man or a woman.

Light and salt – that is who you are. You can't be any of these and shy away from communicating the gospel to the non-Christians. Your inherent character will revolt at your silence when an opportunity for the gospel presents itself. Your constitution will protest at your passivity in front of a life so precious to the Father. The inner force of the real you will not let you rest until you have broken your inertia and initiated that important conversation.

But like in all issues of life, the choice is yours. You can choose to hide behind the wall of busyness or any other such walls. But you can also lift up your head, see the field that is ripe for harvest and put in the sickle.

The Road To Competence

"He has made us competent as ministers of a new covenant—not of the letter but of the Spirit; for the letter kills, but the Spirit gives life." 2 Corinthians 3:6

God's desire is to make us competent ministers of the new covenant. Our competency is not about churning out laws of God to people. Anyone can do that. Competence is in reaching to the heart of men. It is about being adequately prepared to impart lives of people. Take impact out of our communication and we are empty vessels.

The road to competence starts with knowing we have been called to be effective in our communication to the world.

Aptly replying those who ask us about our hope in Christ God wants our words to burn in people's hearts just as they did in the time of Jesus.

Not offending in words requires that we pay attention to a few factors that define our competence as ministers. The factors include *Attitude, Culture, Expectation, Education, Experience, Environment and Emotion.*

It has been said, and very rightly too, that attitude is everything. The attitude we bring into communication with others shapes our words and their impact. We think we can and we can. We believe we are able to sustain a relationship with our words and we have the courage and enthusiasm to speak. We believe the words we speak are life and we feel the power as we communicate. We have the attitude that the Gospel is God's power unto salvation and we are emboldened to step out and preach, even when dogged by a feeling of inadequacy.

Every communication takes place within a cultural setting. Understanding the culture we carry and the culture we are speaking in helps us to recognize turn-offs and turn-ons. There are things we say and do which turn people on and secure their attention. There are others that close their hearts to our communications. Such turn-offs are barriers that cripple even the most honest communication. Most of our communication efforts are now cross-cultural as our cities become cosmopolitan. Diversities also exist with religion, ethnicity, age, sex and status. Even institutions have cultures that distinguish them from the pack. A key ingredient here is to listen, observe and learn as much as you can about the people you are speaking to. Be they colleagues in the office or members of your congregation.

Your expectation of the communication should be realistic and only be as unrealistic as the Holy Spirit will allow. To have high expectation when the Holy Spirit has not signaled us to so do is to court discouragement. Why would you think just one communication with your wife will make her agree to your early retirement? You may wish to spread the communication over a period of time, depending on how you evaluate your wife's attitude to news that border on financial insecurity. How about starting with sharing news about men and women who are retiring early to take on new challenges? Observe her reaction and plan a new communication experience with a new expectation. This may include your new business ideas or the ministry burden God has placed on your mind lately. Do this until you are persuaded she is ready. You may wish to put it in form of a question. "Honey, have you ever seen me retiring early?" To communicate with competence, you must manage your expectation.

A competent communicator must be a life-long learner. Education is key. The broader and deeper your education on issues, the better equipped you are to communicate effectively with others. Like Alvin Toffler advised, you must be willing to 'learn, relearn and unlearn' to stay relevant.

Experience, as we have seen, refers to knowledge of concepts, theories, ideas, facts...acquired by the sender through listening, reading, studying, experimenting, reflecting and experiencing. You must be ever ready to experiment and explore. That makes your experience rich and saves you from being parochial. You will do well to believe that 'all things work together for good for those who are in Christ Jesus'. That will help you put your experiences in divine perspectives and learn from them.

In your speech, environment matters. Should you chastise your wife before the children? Should you rebuke a church elder in public? A hitherto good communication can fail when the speaker fails to consider the appropriateness or otherwise of the environment.

Are you about to communicate with the right emotion? Your speech will fly on the wings of your passion. Enthusiasm and energy will never fail you at any time. But you must moderate your emotion to suit the occasion. Should you show anger or maintain your cool? Should you laugh or smile?

Other factors include: knowledge of the topic, age, and sex, among others. The occasion also affects the coding of the message.

You are beginning to see how complex the communication process is. A speaker has an important role to play in ensuring his communication sails through. We shall consider an important tool he must deploy if he desires to succeed.

09

JOURNEY MERCIES

You ask a man on a journey where he is going. He answers that he does not know. I am sure you will ask in amazement:" So, how would you know when you get there?" If he replies, "I don't know, " I want to believe you will suggest he has a date with his psychiatrist. That underscores the importance of goals.

In a way, every communication is a journey. More specifically, every communication is a voyage. We are journeying in the sea of emotions and attitudes. We are navigating the difficult terrain of human experiences and complex natures. We are rowing against the tide of barriers that seek to submerge the meaning and the intent of our words.

The voyage is vital. It may be the difference between life

and death; between love and hatred; and between hope and despair. If the ship of communication endures the tide and arrives safely to the harbour, it may mean the healing of a relationship or the restoration of a vision. If it capsizes, it may portend the death of a marriage or the drowning of a vision.

One vital way to ensure a safe voyage is to have a clear goal. Like every good sailor answers with precision where he is sailing to, so must a communicator be clear minded as to what he wants to achieve.

With the clarity of destination, a sailor is set to embark on an investigation and preparation that will reduce the incidence of dangerous voyage. He gets weather report. He gets the navigation routes. With these he knows when, where and how to steer the ship. He may need to postpone a voyage until it is safe to journey. He may need to select a route from some alternative routes for safety and or for convenience.

A communicator is not expected to do less. The clarity of the speech goal makes audience and environment analyses easier and speech preparation less labourious. With the knowledge of where you are going comes a focus. Focus helps you devote resources to the speech. It also helps you measure your speech effectiveness.

There are varieties of speech goals. And every communicator must be clear-minded as to what speech goals he is pursuing at any particular time.

You are a political strategist and your client has just lost a vital support in a district. You are before your client to explain why this has happened. You are a medical doctor and a patient had just died on your operating table. You have been invited by your boss to explain how it happened. You are a professional land surveyor and have been called upon by the plaintiff or the defendant's attorney to testify in a land dispute.

In each of these instances your speech goal is to clarify. You are expected to convey information accurately. The goal here is to present hard, unembellished facts. There is no need for whipping up of emotions. No merry-go-round. This is not the time to go for a joke. The objective is to make the listener see. The communicator's effectiveness lies in his ability to present in clear and unmistakable terms the issues at stake.

There was the story of a pastor who was advanced the sum of US $ 5,000 by his church board to facilitate a ministerial trip to the United States. On his return, the board asked him to give the account of his expenditures and retire the balance of the fund advanced. He cleared his throat, raised his hands to heaven and began to recount the mighty outpouring of the power of God during his visit. "God literally showed up," he volunteered. "Never in the history of my ministry have I experienced such a tremendous move of God."

The board was surprised. They thought the pastor did not hear them correctly. One of the members decided to lay the issue squarely on the table. "Pastor, we would like to know how you spent the money advanced to you for your last trip." The pastor looked like a man from the outer space. His silence was ominous. The board members watched the drama with disdain. The pastor took his big Bible and furiously threw it on the floor. With the steps of an angel, he stood firmly on the Bible, laughed heartily and spoke for the first time in minutes, "On this Bible I stand." To which one of the board members responded, "He that thinks he stands should take heed lest he falls." The pastor was voted out of the church.

The pastor's speech backfired because he chose a speech goal that did not fit the occasion. He should have just come up with his expensive report. He was asked to clarify, not to preach.

What happens when you want to show off a new technology that your company has just developed to a potential client? Or when you set out to impress a colleague who thinks your knowledge of the current political situation is deficient? Your speech goal is to impress or inspire. In this case, your communication involves emotional association. Mere seeing is not sufficient; the listener must feel what you feel. Your ability to arouse this feeling is the strength of your communication.

To convince is the goal of a lawyer before a jury or a judge. Same with an evangelist speaking to an audience packed with skeptics of the Christian faith. A wife trying to persuade her husband to go for the third child has a similar goal; just like a daughter who is trying to get her father to pay for a school organized field trip.

Beyond seeing and feeling, the speaker with this goal

wants the listener to accept the subject as truth. This requires a clear and persuasive speech that arouses feelings and elicits acceptance of the issues being canvassed.

Most of the time, the communicator wants to provoke action. The speaker wants the listener to see, feel and accept his point. In addition, he wants the listener to do something about it. In this case the judge is not only convinced, he goes further to acquit and discharge the attorney's client. The audience of skeptics responds to the invitation to make Jesus the Lord over their lives. The wife gets her husband committed to bringing their third child to the world and the persuasive daughter gets her dad to pay for her field trip.

Dominant here is the desire of the speaker to have the audience perform an action as a result of his message.

If you are giving an after-dinner-speech, your goal will be to entertain. The same goal applies when you are with your friends relaxing by the poolside; or when you and your spouse are on a leisure ride on a lonely road to your village. This is every comedian's goal. It is also the goal of a speaker who wants to present a serious issue in a lighter mood or a husband who is looking for a way to apologize and mend fences with his estranged wife.

Most effective communicators pursue this goal at one time or another. The idea here is to amuse, arouse pleasant feelings, interest, mild delights or even hearty laughter.

Goals And Sub Goals

In a typical communication, there may be a main goal and one or more sub goals. A lawyer may have as his goal the discharge and acquittal of his client by provoking the judge to action. He may employ convincing as a sub goal. He may even plan entertainment of the judge as another sub goal. In one presentation, he has three goals – one main goal and two sub goals.

Once I was asked to counsel a young man who was treating his girl friend ungentlemanly. The girl friend had set up an appointment for me to meet the young man, with the hope that I would get him to change his attitude. She informed me the young man was reluctant to see me, wondering what qualified me to counsel with him. He would have preferred having a session with his unmarried pastor than a man with no spiritual qualifications like me. [Just so my readers know, I am a professional and businessman – a minister of God in the marketplace.] I prayed before his arrival, asking the Lord for wisdom on how to approach the encounter.

As he approached me outside our home, it was obvious he did not want to see me. He would neither come in nor take a drink. Besides, he arrogantly announced he would not spend more than fifteen minutes with me.

I knew what my goal was. I would go for convincing the guy of the benefits of being gentlemanly. I would not want to have him commit himself to doing so immediately. That would be a tall order. I could possibly go for that in subsequent meetings. But I also recognized I needed to impress him – to let him accept me as one qualified to counsel with him and to see me as one he could trust. And so, I set as a sub goal to impress him.

To impress him, I tactically flaunted my credentials without sounding overtly arrogant. I mentioned some of the pastors he respected who had either phoned or visited me lately. I asked how long he thought I had been married for? He got it wrong. "Fifteen years," I corrected him, smiling. Then, I went for the clinger: "I thank God that we have been able to help a number of couples and would-be couples along the way. Even then, we are still learning. I would love to learn about things the Lord may be teaching you in this area."

While this was going on, he sat down with me outside our home. At one point, he removed his jacket and requested for a glass of water. As I stood up to get him water, he followed me into the house, asking questions after me. At the end, he accepted the need for women, especially those that are special to men, to be treated with respect. By the time he left, we had spent close to two hours together and he met me several times thereafter.

No journey is worth it without a picture of where you are going. It is foolhardy to do otherwise. Communicating is a journey. It's a special kind of journey that involves sharing your experiences with others. And to ensure journey mercies, you must have a speech goal.

10

GOT A MESSAGE?

What do you have to say? There is no point igniting your vocal chord without a clear message to pass across. The message is the experience you wish to share. Your goal is to help your listener have the same experience. What is this idea? What is your message? It must be clear in your mind what the message is. To be effective, your message must be relevant, beneficial, credible, and owned.

A relevant message passes the suitability test. If it is not suitable to the listener, don't say it. A request for someone that does not own a car to borrow you one is an irrelevant message. The same is true of a salvation message to a minister (assuming the minister is authentic). It is also like preaching to the choir. A relevant message saves time and creates interest.

The goal of Biblical communication is to benefit the listener. If your message is not beneficial, it is of no use. Will this message build up the listener? Will it make him a better person? Will it advance him? Only messages that address these questions satisfactorily stand the chance of benefitting the listener. There is no point whatsoever in trying to sell ice to the Eskimos.

To be effective, the credibility of a message should not be in doubt. Are you sure what you are about to say is the truth and nothing but the truth? If you have a shadow of doubt about the credibility of the message, you will do well to discard it.

You can try but you cannot effectively communicate a message that you have not owned. A dog knows its owner. If you have not made efforts to court and own a message you gleaned from another source, it will bark throughout your effort to transmit it. Think through a message before you share it. Ponder on it till it becomes an experience. Better still, experiment it and prove its veracity. The quality of the message improves with every pondering. Don't rush to share a message you haven't pondered and reflected upon. Make it yours before you share it. You are more confident delivering a message that you own. John demonstrated that in his first epistle.

> *"That which was from the beginning, which we have heard, which we have seen with our eyes, which we have looked at and our hands have touched—this we proclaim concerning the Word of life. The life appeared; we have seen it and testify to it, and we proclaim to you the eternal*

life, which was with the Father and has appeared to us. We proclaim to you what we have seen and heard, so that you also may have fellowship with us. And our fellowship is with the Father and with his Son, Jesus Christ." 1 John 1:1-3

In essence, he was saying, "we are not mere conduit pipes for the message to pass through. We own the message."

Whose Message?

I watched as the preacher laboured hard to get his message across. I could sense in his voice that this was an ill-digested message. He must have gleaned it from a popular preacher's book, from which he quoted copiously. He sweated profusely to convince us of his views, but he failed. He failed because the views were not genuine. In the mouth of the original writer or speaker, they might be. But not this speaker that wanted to reap where he did not sow. The message went flat because it was not owned by the speaker.

Another way of harming your message is to allow a defective experience to colour your message. That was a grouse Jesus had with the spiritual leaders of his days.

"For laying aside the commandment of God, you hold the tradition of men —the washing of pitchers and cups, and many other such things you do...making the word of God of no effect through your tradition which you have handed down. And many such things you do." Mark

7:8, 13 [NKJV]

I once asked a preacher why he allowed himself to be so idolised by his followers, to the extent that about six parishioners were always on guard near the altar whenever he was preaching. His response was quick, "Check 1 Timothy 5:17 and see."

> *"The elders who direct the affairs of the church well are worthy of double honor, especially those whose work is preaching and teaching." 1 Timothy 5:17*

"Thank you, " I said to him in love. "Would you mind to share with me how this tradition started?" He didn't mind telling me. It started with his mentor in the ministry. And now, he has made a doctrine out of it. All his boys were waiting for their time they too would stand on their own and enjoy those priviledges. And the tradition would go on and on.

It is possible for a poor evangelist to present a fragmented picture of Christ; coloured by his own parochial experience and opinions rather than the accurate claims of Jesus.

To ensure your message is not defective, avoid communicating unsubstantiated news or story. Whatever you glean from other sources should be pondered upon until you have come to believe them personally. Do this even for the Bible or for the message from your pastor.

Nevertheless, it is important that the sender owns his

message by taking personal responsibility for the ideas and the feelings he is conveying. Phrases like "*One feels*", "*Most people*", etc do not lend strength and conviction to the speaker's message. In a way, for an evangelist, the gospel of Jesus should become *My Gospel* [Rom. 2:16; 2Tim. 2:8]. Not because he has chosen to write another gospel, but because he has owned the gospel of Christ.

The New Birth – A Process Or An Event?

Did you remember the process you went through in your journey to becoming a Christian? Or, did it all happen in one momentous day? I remember mine. And it didn't happen in one day. I am not in any doubt that my March 13 1976 experience was not an event, but a culmination of a process. As I stood there, head bowed, I could recall a junior student in my High School days come up to me to ask, 'Sir. I was just wondering…have you considered where you would end up should you drop dead today?" That must have been 1974. I recall how hard I struggled to contain my anger and how hard it was for me to forget the question. That question was the first major challenge to me, not more for its content but for the love and audacity that drove the questioner. Before then, I had sneaked into a few Scripture Union squash parties to hear them say things about God and his Son, Jesus. Even though they didn't make sense to me at that time, they ensured I was no stranger to the claims of Christ. A few individual encounters had also taken place that didn't lead to a decision but were all parts of the process that shaped March 13 1976.

THE SPIRIT DECISION PROCESS MODEL (ENGEL)

General Role	Comcation Role		Man's Response
General Revelation		-8	Awareness of a Supreme Being
Conviction	Proclamation	-7	Some knowledge of Gospel
		-6	Knowledge of Fundamentals of Gospel
		-5	Grasp of Personal Implication of Gospel
	Call for Decision	-4	Positive Attitude Toward Act of Becoming a Christian
		-3	Problem Recognition and Intention to Act
		-2	Decision to Act
		-1	Repentance and Faith in Christ
REGENERATION			NEW CREATURE
Sanctification	Follow-up	+1	Post Decision Evaluation
	Cultivation	+2	Incorporation into Church
		+3	Conceptual and Behavioral Growth
External Reproduction			• Communion with God • Stewardship • Internal Reproduction
		Eternity	

Figure 6

The Sprit Decision Model shown in Figure 6 is often credited to James F Engel – a professor at Wheaton Graduate School. This model has since undergone a lot of changes with each version helping us understand aspects of the process better. One of the basic versions is presented here. Whichever version you use gives an understanding of the process leading to a decision for Christ and the aftermath. It depicts the roles of God, the Christian and the non-Christian listener in the communication of the gospel.

This model underscores the importance of the Holy Spirit in the listener's response to the gospel. It is the Holy Spirit that clears the noise that seeks to impact negatively on the communication process. He does all these in cooperation with both the speaker and the listener. It goes to show that our skills are only relevant when they become tools in the hands of the Holy Spirit to bring a non-Christian to conversion.

The model also reveals the need to modify our goals (expectations) and our message to suit the level of preparedness of the listener. Unless the Holy Spirit dictates otherwise, it would be foolhardy to expect a man with no previous knowledge of the gospel to make an intelligent decision for Christ. The message should then be to create awareness about the gospel.

From the model, we obtain information about the readiness of the listener to make a decision for Christ. It's like knowing when to call the harvest. Making an appeal for verdict should not be indiscriminate. It should be done from our understanding of where the listener is on the scale and in conjunction with the Holy Spirit. As in all situations, the Holy Spirit should have the final say.

We had gone out in twos to share the gospel. Even though I was just two years old as a Christian, I was eager to get the gospel message across to as many people as possible. And so, when the opportunity presented itself for Christian students from my university to go out on evangelism, I stuck my neck out. There were like twenty teams of two. I was paired with an older Christian. I think we had two leaders supervising the teams. My team had tremendous success sharing with enthusiastic people. There were first-time decisions and there were dedications. I remember the case of a man that I spoke to. He had had a prior knowledge of the gospel. As we progressed in our conversion, I had a nudge in my spirit to make a appeal for verdict. This infuriated my older Christian, who thought I had not exhausted the steps we had been taught. I pulled the older Christian aside and pleaded with him to please allow me do what I felt led of the Spirit to do. I went ahead and led the man to the Lord. My partner watched with joy. He was affirmed my decision. "I believe we got it right. The Holy Spirit is bigger than any of us."

Appealing For A Verdict

A message, especially, the gospel requires the action of the listener. To leave the listener without the opportunity to make a decision for or about Christ is like a man who stalls a girl for so long and freaks out when it comes to asking her out. It is like a lawyer who puts up a good case but becomes dumb when he needs to make a request of the judge or the jury on behalf of his client. Or, like a salesman that makes a good pitch and shies away from asking for a client's order.

As believers, we are God's sales people. We have the best article any salesman can possibly have. Our product holds a promise of a good life here and in the hereafter. Hopefully, we have experienced the product. Beaming with the joy that our product gives and the hope it imparts, we go forth with confidence to make our pitches. We have big advantages over other salespeople. They have a product designed by man and that which money can buy; we have a product that is made in heaven and that has been fully paid for. Their product may be defective, even with the best care taken in design and production. (And that's not far-fetched considering the number of product recalls in history.) We have a genuine article that cannot be recalled because of defect or, even, deterioration. They have the backing of their company – big or small; we have the backing of God of heaven and the earth. They have the field support of their manager; we have the full real-time support of the Holy Spirit. They are driven by financial gains; we are driven by God's command and by the efficacy of our product. They may or may not have been beneficiaries of their products. (Indeed, how many Ferrari salesmen drive Ferrari? Or, how many Boeing saleswomen own a Boeing?) But we own our product. We know its appeal firsthand. We are not just preachers of the gospel; we are experiencers of it.

> *"We saw it, we heard it, and now we're telling you so you can experience it along with us, this experience of communion with the Father and his Son, Jesus Christ." 1 John 1:3 [MSG]*

After the golden-calf experience, Moses made an appeal, *"Whoever is for the LORD, come to me." [Exodus 32:25].* It was a time of decision and Moses did not shy away from the moment. Joshua followed suit in Joshua 24:15: *"But if serving the LORD seems undesirable to you, then choose for yourselves this day whom you will serve...But as for me and my household, we will serve the LORD."*

Jesus was never one to run away from appealing for a verdict. He constantly asked his listeners to follow him. He said to the fishermen who had not caught fishes all night until he came to their rescue: *"Follow me, and I will make you fishers of men." [Matthew 4:19 KJV]*. To a man who wanted to bury his father before he would follow Jesus, the Lord appealed for a verdict, saying, *"Let the dead bury their own dead, but you go and proclaim the kingdom of God." [Luke 9:60]*

A message is incomplete without a close. The close is the appeal for action being canvassed in the body of the message. It may be an invitation to think differently, follow a different path or take concerted action in a particular direction. The speaker will be deluding himself and wasting his own precious time as well as other's time if he chooses not to bring his message to a conclusion. Of course, the Spirit Decision Model [Figure 6] comes in handy to guide in the types of appeal to make to our listeners. To someone not familiar with the gospel, our appeal may be, "Wouldn't you want to some time reading the Bible?" To someone who has not come to the stage of seeing the implication of the gospel on his personal life, we might want to appeal thus: "Would you like me to pray with you on your needs?" And for the listener we perceive in our spirits to be ready, we should never be ashamed to say, "Would you like, at this moment, to ask Jesus into your life?"

You should be emboldened by the Holy Spirit to make a demand on your listeners to act. It may be to read a book, watch a movie with you, follow you to an event or think through an idea for a later discussion.

CHAPTER

11

THE WORLD
OF WORDS

We are in a world of words. Words play a vital part in the communication of thoughts, ideas and experiences. It's a medium that has been widely used across the ages. It's a medium this book is focused on.

We can only disparage the power of words at the peril of our communication efforts. Our words carry so much power, as we have seen. And the goal of a communicator is to find the powerful word that would impact his listeners. This is how Jesus is upholding all things. It is the only way we too can and make significant impact on our world.

The challenge of communication is that meanings of words and symbols are arbitrary, not universal. We are dealing with a medium that is subject to different interpretations, based on the perceptions of both the speaker and the listener. This calls for care on the part of the speaker, especially. He needs to be aware that his words can be easily misconstrued and his sincere message may fall flat on the account of the challenge of meaning.

I tried out an exercise with a number of sessions I held on communication in the past, to underscore the severity of the challenge of meaning. I pronounced once a short sentence, *"She's hot"*. I asked participants to tell me what they thought I meant. The responses were very instructive and demonstrated in clear terms the challenge of meaning.

Here are some of the responses. "She is beautiful." "She is feeling hot." "She has a fever." "She is sexy." "She is hot-tempered." "She is angry." "She is not happy." Some participants got my pronunciation wrong and thought I actually said, "She is hurt." For that reason they came up with a different set of responses: "She is hurt by something," "She is feeling pain." "Somebody has offended her." "She is sad." "She has been betrayed."

Can you imagine the multiple interpretations a three-word sentence was subjected to? Imagine the huge possibilities of a misrepresentation in a one-hour sermon!

As you must have observed, the multiple interpretations arose not only on the meaning of words but also on the pronunciation. Were you not shocked at how my pronunciation was misunderstood? The truth is that this happens all the time.

Creating Meaning

If creating meaning and understanding is a major purpose of a biblical communication, as we have learned earlier, then the communicator must be concerned about the possibility of the failure of his message on the account of a misunderstood word, phrase or sentence. Communicators have devised various ways of helping their listeners have better understanding of their words. We shall consider a number of them here.

- *Familiar Words*

One of the major ways to ensure meaning is to use familiar words. Really, it is dumb for the speaker to employ high-sounding multi syllables, just so he may prove his knowledge and eloquence. In the world where meaning and understanding do not matter, that would be appropriate, if not celebrated. But not in ours – we have a responsibility to get God's mind out on all issues that pertain to life. God is concerned about meaning, as the Communicator-In-Chief himself. We too must be. So, familiar words should come to the rescue. May I inform here that it is a lot easier to complicate communication than to simplify it? Because we speak as we think, not as we want to be understood. So, it takes effort – real effort – to stick to familiar words.

Wasn't that what Jesus did? His generation was agrarian. So, Jesus used words like seed, shepherd, water, fishes, burden and yoke. He rarely spoke above their heads. He was with them, not only physically but in the familiar corridor of words, needing not much elaboration.

• *Creative Word*

Arranging words skillfully according to the rules of the language is the hallmark of a great speaker. Creativity makes the words come together in a fashion that attracts the audience's attention. For example, speakers deploy the **rule of three** to make their words pungent and their communication attractive.

Wikipedia defines the **rule of three** as "a principle in rhetoric that suggests that things that come in threes are inherently funnier, more satisfying, or more effective than other numbers of things." Example of this rule abound in the Bible as well as writing and speeches across the ages. For example; Father, Son and Holy Ghost; Wake up, Walk, Run; Go, fight, win; Signed, Sealed and Delivered; Pursue, Overtake and Recover."

• *Repetition*

Repetition is yet another way communicators advance meaning. Effective speakers are aware of the word pollution and the many distractions of the listener, so they repeat words, phrases, sentences or even concepts in the course of their speeches to ensure their ideas stick in the listener's mind. How many times did you catch Jesus say, 'Again I say unto you'? The Lord of communication knows how important it is to get his audience's attention.

In rhetoric, there are several kinds of **repetition** where words or certain phrases are repeated for a stronger emphasis by the speaker.

- *Repetition at the beginning of every clause:*
  "We shall fight on the beaches, we shall fight on the landing grounds, we shall fight in the fields and in the streets, we shall fight in the hills* we shall never surrender." (Winston Churchill)
- Repetition at the middle of every clause:
  "We are troubled on every side, yet not distressed* we are perplexed, but not in despair* persecuted, but not forsaken* cast down, but not destroyed..."
- Repetition at the middle of every clause:
  "What lies behind us and what lies before us are tiny compared to what lies within us." (Ralph Waldo Emerson)
- Triad is a set of three sentences with the same or similar beginning or ending, all emphasizing the same theme. Triad is a type of repetition.
- *Repetition of a single word:*
  "Words, words, words." (Hamlet)

Speakers across the ages have learned the creative use of repetition to draw attention to the main points of their speeches.

- ## *Creating Images*

Communicators are aware that experiences are stored in the listener's mind in languageless form, as images. So, they go for words that evoke familiar images at the back of their listener's minds. They run away from abstractions that state information but do not evoke images.

For example, instead of saying, "Sinners will live eternally in hell," they say, "Imagine what's like when you wake up after death to discover your eyes are wide open in a lake of fire, that will serve as your home for ever." Another example is a speaker speaking to a South African audience and desirous to talk about his biking prowess. One speaker might say, "I biked a distance of 1400 Kilometres during this period." That's an abstraction. A more experienced speaker would relate that distance to the image his listeners already have in their minds. So, she goes like, "It's like biking all the way from Johannesburg to Cape Town."

In the words of James Stewart, "*Truth made concrete will find a way past many a door where abstractions knock in vain.*" Effective speakers make their truth concrete by creating images at the back of their listeners' minds.

One of the effective ways of creating images is the use of figure of speech. You learned that in High School; remember? It's time to dust up your notes and put those words in figures that the listeners can identify with.

We use a **simile** to draw attention to similarity between two objects. Similes are typically marked by use of "like" or "as" or "than", or "resembles". Example: *You are like a sheep without a shephered.* Another is: *Without Jesus, you are like a rudderless ship going nowehere but disaster.*

In a **metaphor**, we directly compare seemingly unrelated subjects. Example: *You are a sheep in the midst of wolves.*

The two objects here are you and sheep.

In **personification**, we attribute human characteristics to inanimate objects. A speaker may say, *"As I opened my door, pitch darkness greeted my eyes."* Or, *"My legs said to me, 'We are tired'."* In the cases, we assumed darkness could greet and legs could speak.

Jesus used images skillfully in his days. To communicate his message effectively, he compared *Spirit* with *water*; *evangelist* with *fisher of men*; *sinner* with *lost sheep*; and *kingdom of God* with *Costly Pearl*. We need to do the same.

- ### *The Art Of Story Telling*

Story enlivens your speech. Jesus told stories – so many stories, as if his listeners were little children. Indeed, we all are like children in our love for stories. That looks like one of our childhood innocence we haven't lost. The reason why stories are winners is because they allow the speaker to create images in the minds of their listeners. The stories hit a home run when the listeners can relate with them. When speakers use stories skillfully, they grip their audiences' attention and increase the potentiality of getting their messages across. There are different types of story.

- An **anecdote** is a short tale, often biographical or personal, based on real life with real persons.
- A **parable** is a brief, succinct story with a

moral or spiritual lesson.
- A **fable** is a story where animals and inanimate objects are given human characters.
- A **joke** is a short story told with the aim to create humour and ending with a punch line.

It had been a great evening. The packed hall was not about to lose its patrons. Young people were everywhere, trying to savour the moment. There was food and drinks. There was singing and choreography. There was fun everywhere. Then, the pastor applied the brakes. "The night is far spent, " he said. "We have to stop here so we can listen to a great speaker from out of town." He went ahead to introduce me. As the introduction went on, I saw the disapproval of the audience. They wanted more music, more singing, and more dancing. As I pondered and prayed, I knew unless the Lord helped me there was no way I could keep the audience for the one-hour allocated to me. In my mind, I knew I could engage them for twenty minutes; not more. So, I decided I was going to tell a story. I dropped my Bible and walked briskly to the podium, under a sobering applause.

"Just one story, everyone. Just one story. And only in twenty minutes. That's all I owe you. Not more." I was shocked at the effect. I got ears and hearts. I carefully linked the story to my topic. I landed safely, with astounding results. The pastor and I had a wonderful time of giving thanks to the Lord for turning the meeting around and ending it so effectively like he did.

My counsel to you is to enter the terrain of hard facts from the soft gate of a story. Jesus did it. You too can.

- *Audio Visuals*

A pastor wanted to tell his audience of the need to constantly get filled with the Holy Spirit. Instead of quoting scriptures upon scriptures, he decided to come to church with a big jar of water with a tap, a one litre filled bottle and a basin. He put the larger jar on a table and the basin under it to pick the water draining from the jar. He positioned the filled litre bottle under the tap and opened it. With no place in the litre bottle, the water from the jar overflowed into the basin. The church watched with surprise why pastor wanted to fill an already full bottle. After he had left his anxious audience wondering for a few minutes, the pastor asked, "Any comments?"

Hands went up everywhere. Everyone wanted to know the rationale behind filling up a full bottle. To which the pastor responded, "Isn't that what we do often? We are full of self and yet we expect the Holy Spirit to fill us. Tell me: where in our lives is the space for him to dwell? And yet without the constant in filling of the Holy Sprit, we are on the path of self-destruction."

Tears flowed ceaselessly in the congregation. The pastor allowed the agonizing prayer to go on for some time; then he lifts up the full bottle and says to his sober audience, "What should we do to this bottle that represents you and me?" To which the tear-eyed audience responded, "Empty it!" In obedience to their request, he emptied the bottle, lifted it up again, as if to say, what next? The church got the message and chorused, "Fill it up!"

After filling the empty bottle with the water from the jar, he asked the audience, "Once?" Again, they responded: "Often." "Regularly." "As often as the Spirit leads."

The message stuck. Every time the parishioners think of Holy Spirit and flesh, they remember the constant emptying and refilling of the bottle. And from that picture, they connect with the need for them to constantly deny the flesh of its demands and give way for the Holy Spirit to rule.

What the pastor did was to deploy **Visual Aids**, as a way to creating images at the back of his audience's minds and make them learn a spiritual truth. Talk of making truth concrete.

Did you remember Jesus wanting to teach about servant leadership? The disciples, angling for top positions in the Kingdom wanted to know who would be the greatest. And what did Jesus do?

> *"He called a little child to him, and placed the child among them. And he said: "Truly I tell you, unless you change and become like little children, you will never enter the kingdom of heaven. Therefore, whoever takes the lowly position of this child is the greatest in the kingdom of heaven. And whoever welcomes one such child in my name welcomes me." Matthew 18: 2-5*

What an effective visual aid that was!

Visual Aids include the use of audiovisual equipment like projectors, flipcharts, backdrops and electronic boards. Whatever helps put your words in pictures, whatever allows your audience to hear, see and learn is a visual aid. By so doing, you mobilize the sense of sight to assist the sense of hearing to improve significantly the audience's attention and comprehension. Use it effectively to create images in the back of your listeners' minds.

- *Beyond Words – Communicating Non-Verbally*

We do not only create images with our words, we also do with our non-verbal. Non-verbal constitutes our facial expression, body posture and the tone of voice. A Stanford University study shows that non-verbal constitutes 65% of communication, with words and phrases constituting only 35%. Meaning that we communicate more non-verbally. It implies that non-verbal is capable of reinforcing or altering the meaning of words as intended by the speaker. Ralph Emerson says, *"Who you are speaks so loudly that I can't hear what you are saying."* That underscores the power of non-verbal.

What should you do as a speaker that seek to impact your listeners? Watch your non-verbal cues. Align them to your speech, so they help to reinforce your message. Don't allow your mannerisms, like pulling of hair or nail biting, stand on the way of your message. Maintain eye contact, while giving or receiving communication. Look in between the eyes, not directly in the eyes, as this may give an impression of aggression. Study body languages and adapt them to suit into your various communication situations. Please know that even non-verbal cues are not universal and that accepted body language in one culture or instance may convey a different meaning in another situation or culture

In all you do, don't forget this - the success of your communication is determined largely by the congruence between your verbal and non-verbal cues. For example, you don't talk about love while your face is frozen. Neither do you appear buoyant while giving a eulogy at the burial of a minor.

CHAPTER

12

GIVING AND RECEIVING FEEDBACK

Would You Please Listen?

Why has listening become such a big issue to mankind? Looks like we listen more with our mouths than with our ears, eyes and hearts. We tend to keep our hearts in a state of readiness to speak at the slightest opportunity. In essence, we listen to speak and not to understand the message. Poor listening makes the speaker feel unappreciated and leaves him or her frustrated. The poor listener also loses the meaning of the information being passed; the consequences of which may be dire depending on the urgency and the gravity of the information.

A man's secretary rushes into his office, screaming, "This is important, sir. I know you said not to be disturbed, but..." The boss cut in, "Then don't, even if the house were burning." All the secretary's protestations were countered by angry words from the boss. The secretary left and contacted other staffs and coordinated a response to what she considered an urgent and important issue. In the next thirty minutes or so when the boss was ready to listen, the staffs were gathered in front of his door to commiserate with him over his wife's death. If he had listened to the secretary, he would have heard, "Sir, your wife is having her attack again and she wants you to call the doctor. She seems to have misplaced her cell phone where the doctor's number is. She's been calling you from the house phone and you are not picking. Please call the doctor now!"

"...Let everyone be swift to hear, slow to speak."
James 1:19

This is a divine order. It is a panacea for troubled relationships and the help we need to make that significant impact we have always desired.

There are reasons why we do not listen as much as we should do. There is a perception that the speaker is the king of the communication experience. While it's true that the speaker is an important interacting element in the communication process, he is not more important than the listener, without whom the speaker's role is redundant. How can there be a speaker without a listener? It is foolhardy to think a listener's role is inferior to that of a speaker. The listener, by the way, writes the report card to the speaker's communication activity. The *Intended Effect* the speaker intends to create is only achieved to the level of the *Actual Effect* attained by the listener. In a sane world, the listener should be given the same treatment a discerning company gives to its choice customers.

So, listen. And, please, listen effectively. There are five levels of listening we operate on. When we are not interested in a message and we do not want to talk about it, we simply show our disinterest by ignoring the listener. We move to the pretending level when we fake a listening activity, deceiving the listener. Both levels of listening are disrespective to the listener and are a sheer waste of the speaker's time. If the message is too long and / or we are pressed for time, we do selective listening, cherry-picking the parts of the message we like to hear while discarding the rest.

There was the story of a wife who told her husband, *"Honey. Please go and drop off the children at school at eight. Don't forget to open the door for the plumber – he needs to drain the sink; you know that. And by the way the garbage can is full and needs to be moved to the frontage for a pickup. You may wish, thereafter, to have some rest, so you can be alert while babysitting later in the day. Love you."*

By the time the wife came back, the children were still at home and husband was resting, because he had heard or had chosen to hear, *"Honey, Please, Go And Get Some Rest."* Now, you are not laughing: are you? As an exercise, try and locate each of the words the husband heard in the wife's message. That was selective listening.

It can be as dangerous as half education. Acting on such information can put lives and relationships in jeopardy.

Good listeners operate on the levels of attentive listening and emphatic or empathetic listening. Attentive listeners give undivided attention to the words and the body language of the speaker. The listener maintains good eye contact and is committed to hearing what is being said. Here, the listener understands and reflects the feelings of the speaker. The listener treats the speaker with utmost regard, talks less and gives verbal and non-verbal feedback to ensure he understands the feeling and the words of the speaker. This is the deepest type of listening. It involves entering the frame of mind of the speaker. Emphatic listening becomes necessary especially when the sharing has a strong emotional content, when the listener is not certain he understands the speaker and when the listener is in doubt the speaker feels confident he is been listened to.

- ### *What good listeners do*

They are *verbally passive and non-verbally active*. They speak less but demonstrate with their bodies that they are getting the message. They choose non-verbal cues that assure the speaker they are listening and are getting the message. They *acknowledge* what they have heard verbally and non-verbally. They nod or just say, "Yes, I got that." They deploy *door openers* to encourage the speaker to continue, using statements like, "Would you like to tell me more about your experience?" Sometimes, they *content paraphrase* in their own words what the speaker has said, to be sure they got it right and to assure the speaker they are getting the message. They might say, *"So, you are saying that you cannot become a Christian because you have been disappointed by the lifestyle of your Christian wife?* In *active listening response,* the listener combines the content paraphrase and the feeling of the speaker. *"You said that you did not like what your wife said to you. Did it make you feel upset?"*

The day has just ended. James is in a hurry to get out of the office and be home early enough to take Helen, his wife for dinner. John – a colleague, on sighting James, runs to him and asks for a car ride to a convenient place. James, as a responsible Christian man, obliges. The two ride quietly for sometime. Under his breath, James asks the Lord to give him an entrance into John's heart, as he prepares to engage him in a conversation. "So, how is your family? Like me, you can't wait to get home to take madam out for dinner?" In the next thirty minutes, James listens – verbally passively and non-verbally actively – as John talks about the problems in his family. It is an emotionally charged experience full of twists and turns of betrayal and of bad choices. James, still praying under his breath, listens emphatically, responding sparingly through door openers and content paraphrases. Before John drops off, he thanks James profusely for listening without judging him. He wonders if he can talk some more with him on the issue. "Sure," as James drives towards home, thankful that he has been a good listener and trusting the Lord to use the opportunity to turn John's life and marriage around.

Here are a few guides to effective listening:

- Accept the speaker's message unreservedly until proved otherwise
- Talk sparingly, speaking only while consenting or seeking for clarification
- Listen attentively and empathetically without preoccupying your mind with how to respond or with other issues.
- Use silence skillfully. Avoid the temptation to fill every silence with words.
- Maintain eye-to-eye contact, where possible. James couldn't have done this while driving.
- Manage your non-verbal cues to ensure they convey your empathy and attentiveness.

What's In A Feedback?

Whether speaking or listening, you need to give or receive feedback or both. Speakers need to ask for feedback to let them know how effective they have been in their communication. Listeners need to give feedback to assist the speaker and to ensure their own understanding of the message

In interpersonal relationship, feedback is a way we affirm and make others feel rewarded for their behaviour or to assist them to make changes for more effective behaviour. It is a tool often deployed by leaders to help others change their lives. It's a veritable tool for evangelism.

While we are tempted to sermonize, sympathize, moralize, praise, advise, ridicule or question the non-Christian or anyone else for that matter, the best approach might be to help him deal with his problems while providing Christ as a viable alternative.

Has anyone wondered why Christians have few non-Christian friends? We tend to sermonize at every opportunity we have. Sermonizing is not synonymous with witnessing for Christ. We sermonize when we feel compelled to share a scripture at every meeting. Confronting with scriptures has a way of finality to it. The listener tends to avoid the discussion, either because he doesn't want to offend the scriptures or because he is pissed off. Sermonizing may project us as not being rational or objective. An average person will like to maintain a decent conversation without the invoking of a higher power – at least, at the beginning. It is important we know that the scriptures challenge men's unrighteousness. It may be a stumbling block to the sharing of our faith if the scriptures are insensitively quoted at the initial stage of a communication experience. When used appropriately, the scriptures remain the best guide for life and vehicle for the transformed life.

Mariam was elated that Adamu – her husband of fifteen years – had finally agreed to meet her pastor for counselling on the challenges he was facing in his finances. Adamu was warmly welcome to the pastor's office by the secretary. Promptly, the pastor was informed of his arrival. Adamu, ever so prompt, had arrived on schedule. He expected the man of God to respect him by being punctual too. For ninety excruciating minutes Adamu waited for the pastor. He must have glanced at his watch for more than twenty times. He took an excuse from the sympathetic secretary to just walk around the area for a few minutes. It was his way of killing boredom. He had hardly reached the road when the secretary joyfully announced the pastor was ready to see him.

He entered the expansive office with trepidation of what to meet being not a Christian. The pastor greeted him with an apology as he motioned him to a seat.

"So, what can I do for you, sir?" The question came too suddenly for Adamu. He had expected a longer and more sincere apology. And now, no pleasantries. Shouldn't he have known what I came here for? The pastor was still looking at some papers, when he lifted up his head, as if to say, "Yes, please."

"I am Mariam's wife. I..."

"I already know that. What's that your challenge again?

"I thought Mariam has told you, sir."

"I have been told a lot of things by many people. I can't keep track of them all. I apologize. I think I remember it has to do with your finances."

"Yes, sir. I would…"

"I believe your case is simple. You have been unfaithful to the Lord and to your wife. It's natural for God to visit you with a financial drought. If you would repent and turn from your wicked ways, God will visit you with abundance. Alleluia!"

The pastor continued on his monologue while still engrossed on the report he was reading. At some point, he thought it was time to lay hands and receive help for Adamu. So, he lifted up his head to discover Adamu was not there. His secretary later confirmed Adamu had left in annoyance. To which the pastor responded, "Imagine what impatience and pride can do in the life of a man!" The pastor then asked for the next person. In her mind, the secretary thought, "Next victim you wanted to say, pastor?

May be it's not as bad in your own environment. But the above story gives us a peep into the minds of ministers who see the listeners as inferior to them. They rarely listen. They enter into quick judgement. They scare people away from the truth. They make no impact on people's lives.

"Do not judge, or you too will be judged."
Matthew 7:1

When we judge others, we are also judged. I judging others, we take the place of God. And God frowns at that. Besides, judging is a frontal attack on people's values. They either recoil to their shells or they fight back. Adamu didn't want to fight; he just walked away, preferring his sorry state to being humiliated. If our goal is to impact, then we must eschew judging others and be more concerned about understanding the rationale behind their belief and behaviour.

Advice is cheap. It is too cheap that it's worthless. It's not the most effective way of giving feedback. It is good to know that you do not possess the power to change others. At best, you can only help them connect with God to change their own lives. Once we know this, our goal would be to help others identify their problems, consider their alternatives and make the best decision under God. This process may be labourious, but it's your best option at impacting lives. Telling people how to live their lives may be the norm, but it destroys individual initiatives and strangulates their capacities to maintain personal contact with God to solve their own problems. Pretending to possess a magic wand to solve human problems may win you a crowd, but it damages your credibility and reduces your level of impact.

This does not mean we should engage in flattery and deny people to the truth. There is no point of being dishonest in your feedback, just so you may curry someone's favour. If Elisha did not flatter Namaan – as highly placed as he was, God would not expect us to flatter anyone. Flattery doesn't bring about transformation, it just makes people's heads to swell to the point that they think they don't need God. There are ways of communicating the truth with minimal offence.

- ### *Some useful guides on Feedback*

  - Be specific
  - Describe behaviour, do not evaluate the person
  - Focus on behaviour that the receiver can do something about
  - Use feedback not to punish but to assist the person towards a better behaviour
  - Give positive feedbacks three times more than negative feedbacks.

You are giving a *specific* feedback you say to your colleague in the office, "Mark. I deeply appreciate your desire to know more about the Lord, especially that you have decided to read the Bible yourself." Here you have specified what his desire to know the Lord that you appreciate. If you say to a friend, "I wish you had listened to me and not have divorced your wife," you are focusing on a behaviour he cannot do something about. He has already divorced his wife. And reminding him of your former advice is unnecessary. A better way to say that would be, "I know you and I discussed the issue about your divorce before you went ahead with it. It would seem you are now regretting that decision. I understand your feeling. What do you plan to do going forward and how do you think I can be of help?"

"Darling you can never change. You will also pick on me. That's what you have done from our first day of marriage." If you say that to your spouse, you are foreclosing any change towards a better behaviour. You are using your communication to punish and not to build up. A better approach is, "Honey, I don't think you intentionally set out to hurt me by picking on me. But each time you concentrate on my shortcoming, I feel bad, sometime worthless. I don't believe this is your goal. Is there a way I can help you improve in this area?"

"You know what I think about you? I think you are a failure. Pure and simple." Many things are wrong with this kind of communication. One, it doesn't build up the listener. By now, I believe, you have seen the need to build your listeners up according to their needs. Secondly, you have evaluated the person of your listener instead of his behaviour. When you evaluate people, you make them feel worthless, even if that's not your original intention.

• *Sandwich approach*

Would you like to have a sandwich? Let's see if you are qualified to have one. Let's assume you have just done something annoying to me. Because I value your friendship, I have decided to let you know about it in the spirit of Christ in me. My goal is to communicate to you this behaviour with, giving you a minimum offense to abandon our relationship. Then, you are qualified to have one sandwich on me.

A typical sandwich has two outer layers and one inner layer. The inner layer is your annoying behaviour that I have decided to communicate to you. Knowing how difficult it is for people, including me, to accept negative feedback, I have chosen to sandwich the negative feedback in between, at least, two positive feedbacks. So, I go like, "I am always thankful to God for having you as a colleague in the office. You have helped me through some of my difficult times in my profession. Thank you. That's why I am isolating a recent experience, where you mentioned in public information that I shared with you in secret. It hurt me so much that I cried. Knowing you, I have no doubt that you didn't go all out to hurt me and would do everything possible to prevent such occurrence in future. Thank you for your time."

I hope you like my sandwich. Go ahead; give sandwiches instead of handing down judgments on people's behaviour.

Seeking Clarifications

Jesus was surrounded by the multitude of people as he concluded plans to leave Jericho. Then a shrieking and desperate noise came from a blind man, Bartimaeus. *"Jesus, Son of David, have mercy on me!"* After overcoming many obstacles, he finally found himself in front of Jesus. What Jesus did was instructive. Instead of laying hands, he asked a question: *"What do you want me to do for you?"* To which he replied, *"Rabbi, I want to see."*

The Lord of lords didn't act on impulse. He sought clarifications. And when he had gotten his response, he acted.

> *"Go," said Jesus, "your faith has healed you." Immediately he received his sight and followed Jesus along the road. Mark 10:52*

In Mark 8:27, he asked his disciples, *"Who do people say I am?"* and followed it up with another two verses later: *"But what about you...Who do you say I am?"*

These are not the only occasions that Jesus asked questions in the Bible. Jesus used questioning skills to obtain information and seek clarifications. Effective questioning helps assure the speaker of our attention. They provide us with valuable information to assist us in the task of helping the speaker to solve his own problems.

- ### *Types of questions*

There are three types of questions communicators use.

- **General** (or broad or open-ended) questions are often used to get the speaker talking about his problem. Example: *Could you tell me about the problem?*
- **Specific** questions are used to pinpoint specific information within a general area. Example: *"How long have you been having this problem?*
- **Close-Ended** questions require a Yes or No. They should be avoided, as they tend to interrupt the flow of information sharing.

13

EMPOWERED COMMUNICATION

Jesus said to her, *"Go, call your husband and come back." [John 4:16]*

The Samaritan woman looked apprehensively to the man before her, saying to herself, "that's a sore point, preacher man. It's a no go area." So, she lied. "I have no husband." That encounter made her see herself in a new light. The light of God had shined in her heart. The man before her was no longer an ordinary man; his message no ordinary message. It was time to call out the whole village to come and see what he had just seen.

It was the Aha moment of Jesus' communication with the Samaritan woman in the fourth chapter of the Gospel of John. This is the moment every communicator looks forward to. It is the moment when his communication with another reaches its peak. Commonality has been established and the listener's eyes glow with the understanding of the message being communicated. It is the moment when a non-Christian realizes the futility of living without Christ and the joy of forgiveness. It is the moment when your spouse agrees to a second child or when your boss sees the need to compensate you more.

To us believers, it is a moment of miracle – a time of divine intervention. A moment to cherish, being the consummation of what we have canvassed for and a reward of our communication effort. This empowered communication is needed in this age and time. Without Jesus coming to the scene and altering the dynamics of the communication, we stand no chance of building up others and impacting our world.

The Aha moment is when we discover the *powerful word* needed to sustain our communication experience. You will recall that the Bible talks about Jesus 'sustaining all things by his powerful word.' [Hebrews 1:3] Communication is about searching for that *powerful word* and the Aha moment is when we do.

This Aha moment comes as the Lord brings a scripture, question, story, song or incidence to our minds. It's a divine leading that changes the tone and the direction of the communication with others. It's the work of the Holy Spirit. It's a moment to treasure. Remove this moment from communication and all you have left is a shell – empty and inconsequential.

Getting To The Aha Moment

The road to the Aha moment is paved with righteousness, prayer and sensitivity to the Holy Spirit. As communicators, we are agents of change. And as we have observed, change is herculean to achieve. Only the Holy Spirit can adequately prepare the hearts of men for them to get to the point of deciding to turn their lives over to Jesus. This divine encounter will not come through skill alone. The challenge of humanity is spiritual. The physical, social, psychological, political, economic and other challenges are but consequences of the spiritual depravity. It's the anointing – working along with our skills – that moves people to the point of vulnerability where they accept the fact of their sinful nature. It is the anointing that breaks the yoke of sin and frees them up to live holy and righteous lives.

> *"And it shall come to pass in that day, that his burden shall be taken away from off thy shoulder, and his yoke from off thy neck, and the yoke shall be destroyed because of the anointing." Isaiah 10:27 [KJV]*

In the same first chapter of Hebrews, quoted earlier, the Bible gives us the secret behind the powerful word of Jesus that sustains all things.

> *"You have loved righteousness and hated wickedness; therefore God, your God, has set you above your companions by anointing you with the oil of joy." Hebrews 1:9*

It's a call on us to live out the nature of God on the inside of us and be true to the Gospel that we preach. Where there is a contamination of sin in our lives, we lose the power of conviction, our words will lack the anointing and our impact will be compromised.

Praying before and during the communication process helps to prepare the hearts of men and sharpen our sensitivity to the Holy Spirit.. Jesus rose up early while it was still dark to pray [Mark 1:35]. Now, we know when those powerful words were crafted and while he remained united with his Father throughout his earthly ministry. Through self-talk, we can maintain a prayerful mood that opens us up to the prompting of the Holy Spirit. Praying in tongues before and during (under our breath) the communication effort helps us to speak mysteries, with consequences of enhancing our faith and calling God into play.

Communication – The Jesus Style

Before the Aha moment of Jesus, there had been a preparation that was a superb combination of skills and the anointing.

Jesus had had to rush out of Judea, for a much needed breather after the Pharisees were infuriated at seeing many people baptized under Jesus' ministry than under the ministry of John who they had clamped in prison. To reach Galilee, he had to pass through Samaria. Tired from travel, hungry, thirsty and wondering why men were against the truth instead of for the truth, he sat by Jacob's well in Sycar – a town in Samaria.

With these challenges facing Jesus, would anyone expect a divine encounter just a few moments away? That's the paradox of our lives. Great things happen when the devil strikes at the heart of our joy- when to complain and murmur seem justifiable, when it is natural to lose hope, and when to share the Good News is way out of our consideration. In these moments of despair, effective communicators unleash the power of their self-talk to encourage themselves in the Lord. They do this, first, to restore their peace, and second, to prepare themselves for possible divine opportunities the Lord might bring their way. I can imagine Jesus encouraging himself as he sat by the well; a burst joy exploding in his heart. All of a sudden, he was assured of his place in history. He was still the Lamb of God to take away the sins of the world. The Gospel he came to preach would reach the ends of the world and he would welcome many sons and daughters into glory. All of a sudden, his tiredness, hunger and thirst paled into insignificance. His peace was intact. It was noon. And he was ready.

- *Vulnerability*

"When a Samaritan woman came to draw water, Jesus said to her, "Will you give me a drink?" [His disciples had gone into the town to buy food.]" Verses 7-8

Jesus ventured out of his shell. He could have let the woman be. After all, he had his own troubles. When we are most vulnerable, we think less of others and God. But that's when histories are written and re-written. Because it is those moments we operate more on the Feeling or

Encounter level, as we risk our vulnerability.

Jesus did not only venture out, he exposed himself further by requesting for water. This was one request the woman might turn down, increasing Jesus' vulnerability. Jesus did not mind. We too must not allow the fear of rejection rob us of a divine encounter.

> *"For the Spirit God gave us does not make us timid, but gives us power, love and self-discipline." 2 Timothy 1:7*

- ### *And the barriers came down*

Being vulnerable was one barrier down – there were many more that came down. There was the *social barrier.* Jesus and her listener belonged to different social classes. He might not be rich but he had dignity; the woman before her possibly shared the poverty status but certainly not the dignity. Again, there was the *religious barrier.* They had their spiritual differences that dated back several years. There was the *ethnic barrier* as Samaritans and the Jews were at loggerhead and the mutual distress and hatred ran deep. The *moral barrier* was pronounced. One was a moral leader, the other a moral wreck. By her lifestyle, she could be a whore.

Jesus broke them all. Whatever it takes, we too should be prepared to pull down barriers militating against our communication effort. Our goal of impacting the world rests on our ability to level up with our listeners, not to distance ourselves from them. Identification with our listeners is the pathway to building common grounds – an essential prerequisite for effective communication. And Jesus has led the way through incarnation – the highest level of identification known to man. Jesus became us when he took on the form of man. We cherish that identification because it was effective in helping us believe in him.

Paul also had his own identification tag, firmly etched on his heart.

> "*Even though I am free of the demands and expectations of everyone, I have voluntarily become a servant to any and all in order to reach a wide range of people: religious, nonreligious, meticulous moralists, loose-living immoralists, the defeated, the demoralized—whoever. I didn't take on their way of life. I kept my bearings in Christ—but I entered their world and tried to experience things from their point of view. I've become just about every sort of servant there is in my attempts to lead those I meet into a God-saved life. I did all this because of the Message. I didn't just want to talk about it; I wanted to be in on it!" 1 Corinthians 9:19-23*

We too must have ours etched on our hearts, if we ever want to make the difference to the world.

• *Dare to engage*

Jesus engaged the Samaritan woman. He didn't lecture. He didn't sermonize. He didn't judge her. Neither did he give her an advice. Instead, he engaged her intellectually and emotionally. He didn't just pull out the Gospel from his sleeves, he contextualized it. He started from water to build a case for the Gospel. He allowed dialogues. He didn't object to being queried, even being antagonized. He listened. He spoke. He answered her questions – all but one. Jesus dodged the ethnic question. It was no use. From water, he skillfully moved to the living water. He made his listener thirst for that water. At some point, she wanted it. She wanted it badly. You would think Jesus would rush to give it. No. She wasn't ready for the altar call. No. not yet. It would be premature. Jesus was waiting for the right moment. Eventually that moment came.

Jesus said to her, *"Go, call your husband and come back." [John 4:16]*

That was it. The Spirit of God had taken the communication to the climax. A woman was on her way to the Kingdom. But it was not only that lady. The whole village was ready. The Samaritan woman's testimony had won many others. The erstwhile woman of easy virtues had become a moral rallying point. Only the Spirit of God could have done that.

14

IN THE GLARE
OF THE PUBLIC

It Was Allan

He stood up to talk. It was his first since he became a Christian. In fact, his first ever. He had always avoided speaking in public. He considered himself a poor speaker, even though he was almost at the zenith of his career. Asked why he hated public speaking with a passion. "I would not want to make a mess of myself," he once confided in his wife.

He took a look at the over one hundred pairs of eyes riveted on him and immediately, his knees began to knock noisily against each other. Then he looked down. It was a grave mistake. He just never wanted to look up again. He held the podium tightly, as if his balance was in danger without it. All along, the unsuspecting audience was clapping at his every move. In the audience were a few friends and acquaintances. The man, through whom he came to know the Lord, was also there. It was a Full Gospel Business Men's Fellowship International's dinner meeting for eminent personalities.

Encouraged by his newfound communication with God, he prayed silently; "Dear Lord. I need your help. I need it now!" He forced his head up, as he struggled with beads of sweat that had enveloped his face. He tried to smile. The people clapped some more. His conversion to Christianity had taken Dan's friends and foes by surprise. One of them was Allan – a High School buddy – with whom he shared some of the escapades he now stood against. Allan had accepted the invitation to the dinner because he wanted to know why. It was a betrayal of some sort for Allan. He and Dan had sworn never to have anything to do with the brand of Christianity that his friend now represented. He stood there silently. He didn't join in the clapping; he just wanted hear Dan out. He had better had good reasons, he thought to himself. Otherwise…

Then, Dan began. Five minutes into his speech, he began to feel good. He even paused a little bit for his audience to take in what he had just said. The knees were now silent, even though he could still hear his own breathing.

A main speaker came up after Dan and literally centred his message on Dan's testimony. After his twenty-minute message, he appealed for a verdict. As he got to that point,

Dan started to cry, asking the Lord to reach Allan. That was one person, apart from his family, that he thought he owed an explanation. The two had avoided each other since Dan's conversion. Dan even had to send the invite instead of talking to Allan about it. He was glad that he came. But will he give his life to Christ? O, Lord. Please open his heart of understanding. Reach him the way only you can, dear Lord.

As about thirty people came out to commit their lives to the Lord, Dan's head was still bowed. Then, slowly, he lifted up his head and immediately moved it around furiously, looking for his friend. Disappointed at not seeing Allan, he said to the Lord, "I guess it's not his time yet, Lord." Then, the new Christians started to file out of the hall to an adjoining room for counselling. One of the men that had been on his knees all along stood up to join the others. His teary eyes and the unsteady walk first caught Dan's attention.

It was Allan.

Out In The Cold?

Many would compare speaking in public with being left in the cold. Away from your comfort zone, you are left all alone in this world to paddle your own canoe and to answer your father's name.

Who can survive that? I hope it won't burst your bubble to know that many men and women across the ages have embraced public speaking as a way of life. What we hate, some love with an undying passion. What we deride, some celebrate with audacity. What we shy away from, some seek every available opportunity to do.

Why has one man's poison become another man's meat? I think the answer is in the benefits of standing up in public to speak. The advantages far outweigh the disadvantages; the glory surpasses the challenge; the honour outstrips the fear. If public speaking is like jumping in the cold, then, there must be large and enduring warmth waiting behind the brief moment of cold.

Through the Greeks came the advent of rhetoric, with the famed Greek Fantastic Four – Aspasia, Socrates, Plato and Aristotle – at the vanguard. Then, the Romans like Cicero and Quintilian perfected the art. And since then, there had been devotees through the Medieval, the Renaissance, the Enlightenment…till the modern day.

This book started with the speech of Jesus. Our Lord relished speaking to many as much as he did speaking to one. He knew both have their places. With one person, he could make that significant impact that changed the life of his listener. Like it was with the Samaritan woman. And with the crowd, he could challenge many to consider aspects of his claims and alter their thinking. He could even astound them with his divine wisdom, leading to either conviction or a desire to know more.

> *"On the Sabbath he began to teach in the synagogue. Many people were there; and when they heard him, they were all amazed. "Where did he get all this?" they asked. "What wisdom is this that has been given him?" Mark 6:2*

Peter was there at the Pentecost. *"Then Peter stood up with the Eleven, raised his voice and addressed the crowd..." [Acts 2:14]* The result was astounding: *"When the people heard this, they were cut to the heart and said to Peter and the other apostles, "Brothers, what shall we do?"" [Acts 2:27]*. Over three thousand people were added to the Church in that one speech.

Paul gave passionate speeches that challenged and amazed his audience. In Athens, a group of Epicurean and Stoic philosophers began to debate with him. Then they took him and brought him to a meeting of the Areopagus, where they said to him, *"May we know what this new teaching is that you are presenting?* Paul did not let them down. He stood up in the midst of the hall and said: *"People of Athens! I see that in every way you are very religious."[Acts 17:22]* At the end of the speech, Paul had a divided house. A group sneered at him. A group would want to hear him some other time. A group believed and followed his teachings. Among the latter group were Dionysius and Damaris.

Before King Agrippa, Paul presented an articulate defense of his faith. On the prompting of the King, *"Paul took the stand and told his story." [Acts 26:1 MSG]* His speech dazed governor Festus and challenged King Agrippa, who said, *"Keep this up much longer and you'll make a Christian out of me!"[Acts 26:28]*. Earlier on, he had scared the corrupt Festus' predecessor – Felix – with his speech.

Stephen, a man given to the Holy Spirit, did many great wonders and miracles among the people. So much that opposition mounted against him. At every turn, Stephen was too much for them. *"But they could not stand up against the wisdom the Spirit gave him as he spoke."* *[Acts 6:10]*. And in Acts 7, he gave a scathing speech that made the Sanhedrin furious and gnash their teeth. That speech earned him the place of being the first martyr of the new Faith.

Good speakers don't leave their audiences the same. You are either for the faith or against it. Speeches engage the mind and the heart. The emotional association to a speech can make listeners cry in repentance or take up cast stones on the speaker. You cannot be indifferent. Such speeches advance the Kingdom as they have done over the ages.

Public speaking is the process of speaking to a group of people in a structured, deliberate manner intended to inform, influence, or entertain the listeners. As you hone your speaking skills and make them available to the Holy Spirit, your listeners may be informed, influenced or entertained. With the possibility being astounded, challenged and convicted.

It's A Command

The apostles had just been released as the angel of the Lord opened the prison doors and brought them out and said to them,

> *"Go to the Temple and take your stand. Tell the people everything there is to say about this Life." Acts 5:20 [MSG]*

It was a command. They were to go to where the people were – at this time, the temple. Taking a stand requires confidence – the type that Jesus and Paul displayed. The angel didn't want anything less. As representatives of the Most High, they should not be afraid of mere men. Their message was to cover the entire spectrum of human existence – *everything to say about this life.*

Regardless of your discipline, God commands you to take your stand and speak out. There is ample opportunity in every discipline to present Christ to the dying world. There is opportunity every field of human endeavour to make the claims for Christ – right in the public square where minds are changed and opinions are moulded. To shy away from the public square is to abdicate the court of public opinion to the devil and his cohorts. Our responsibility has light and salt will be hindered. And so is God's plan for us to disciple the nations.

We must bring God to the public domain whenever the opportunity presents itself.

The Fear Factor

Fear of public speaking is reportedly one of man's greatest fears. We saw it in Dan. Dan is no stranger to many across the world. How many opportunities to advance the Kingdom have we allowed to slip by because of fear. Fear is crippling. Even then, fear should be understood, not dreaded. It should be understood, as *"nameless, unreasoning, unjustified terror which paralyzes needed efforts to convert retreat into advance."* [Franklin D. Roosevelt]

Seeing fear as it is reduces the dread of fear. Fear is nothing but a signal similar to the one you have when you are about to navigate a voyage. It's normal to have trepidation of a voyage. It's normal to ask: Will everything be okay? Experience has shown that confidence in speaking comes with a well-practiced speech tailored to a well-researched audience. Drawing from past experiences, if we have any, or from our preparations, if we are newcomers can ameliorate this fear. Good speakers do a lot of self-talking to assure themselves that speaking is like a voyage and that this voyage will go well, like many others before it. Newcomers try to simulate life speechmaking situations before their speech. They deliver their speeches to family and friends. They stand before their mirrors and imagine their audiences seated. Happily, the mind has no way of knowing these are not real-life. And so, when fear comes, as it always will, they rely on their 'past experiences' to ameliorate the impact of fear.

It's important to note that fear never goes finally away before the speech. Even the best of speakers feel the infamous butterfly in their stomachs. What do they do? First, they are well prepared, having researched their audience well and having rehearsed their speeches over and over. Second, they own their opening statements. Some memorize their opening lines. The fact that they don't have to think about their opening statements reduces their trepidation. Third, they just keep on acting as if they are not afraid. They look at the audience with practiced (not real) confidence, knowing that the fear won't last. Just as we saw in Dan's speech at the dinner meeting. Fourth, they pray. Knowing that Heaven backs you to bring some comfort. Talking to God about your fears, gives you peace on the inside. It builds up your faith and sets you up for the encounter. Realising this is a spiritual battle helps you situate the fear appropriately. There is an enemy out there, who will play on this natural fear to frustrate your speech. As you align yourself with God, you frustrate the plan of this enemy and receive the divine strength to fight a good fight of faith over the souls of men.

Deep breathing and a couple of exercises have been known to help reduce tension. But none of these is as important as a good preparation.

Preparing For The Voyage

So, you have been asked to speak at the Old Student's Association Dinner? Let's assume it's your version of Dan's speech. They haven't given you any topic. They just want you to speak for thirty minutes on any topic of your choice. What do you do?

The first thing that comes to the minds of most newcomers is to labour over the topic and research. This usually wears them down. Some give up at this time.

- *Brainstorm, Pray*

Sit back to pray and think. Find out what suits you best. A walk in the park or a gaze at the ceiling? I have a friend who gets ideas for his speeches on a long walk in his community. There is another who feels most comfortable thinking away while seated on the toilet bowl. Whatever makes you meditate, sensitive to the Sprit and think – do it.

The beauty of this stage is that you unleash the power of the Holy Spirit to remind you of things you would not otherwise remember. You might recall stories of your school years that challenged you to think differently and formed the foundation of your success. You might encounter funny stories that would make them laugh. With a tablet or a write pad, try and write down all the ideas as fast as you can. You don't have to bother about grammar and even sense. Just write.

In the end, you come up with ideas that are authentically yours. Remember you can only communicate with confidence ideas that you have brooded upon and that have become authentically yours.

As you progress, ideas begin to shape in your mind. The Holy Spirit is at work, putting your thoughts together. A direction emerges. May be a couple of directions. More pondering helps you determine the best direction.

- *What is your topic?*

In selecting your topic, please note the following:

- *Select topic on issue you have knowledge or experience about.*
- *Ownership of a message is essential for confident and life-transforming delivery.*
- Give a heading that will appeal to the audience. Instead of *Recalling Our Days Back In High*

School, think of something more creative and appealing like, *When Men Were Boys.*

• *Gathering Information*

There are several sources of information that include; the Bible, the Internet, and your experience. It is important not to interfere with the flow of information. As the Holy Spirit reminds you of a scripture, an idea or an experience, put it down, even if you are on something else. If your tablet or notepad is not around, record it anywhere, including your palm, napkin or tissue paper. Speakers are aware they are often not able to recall a fleeting but important idea they failed to record. Wouldn't that leave your information scattered? Yes; but you don't have to be worried about that. Creativity does not usually subject itself to structured environment. In essence, creativity thrives in organized chaos.

Once you are done with information gathering, begin to piece together your chaotic recordings. You are ready for the next stage of structuring your speech.

• *Structuring your speech*

How would you want your speech structured? There are various ways of doing this. Let's consider two of them. You can reduce your speech to three segments as follows

- Tell them what you wish to tell them
- Tell them
- Tell them what you have just told them

This simple structure supports all kinds of speech. The beauty of this structure is in the creativity with which you handle each segment. You may open with, *"Today, hope has gone through the roof. We have witnessed the death of hope and have sunk into despair. Can we bring hope back? I believe we can. And that's the reason I am here today."* That is more creative than for you to say, *"Good morning. Today, I am going to tell you how to restore hope."*

Another structure is the simple one you are, I believe, accustomed to from your elementary school days.

- Introduction [Also called the Opening]
- Body [Main thrust of your message. The reason the listeners are gathered.]
- Summary [Also called Conclusion. Appeal for a verdict. Recap of your main points. What you want them to remember or do. Your final word.]

- ***Drafting and delivery***

With information available to you, start with a draft of your speech. You may or may not have to read it, depending on the occasion and your preference. At least, it's a good practice to have your ideas written down in the sequence that you want them. In drafting your speech, the acronym AIDA can come in useful.

AIDA

Arrest Attention	Attention-gripping statements or pictorial
Create Interest	What excites the listener? What is capable of getting him out bed in a windy stormy night?
Arouse Desire	What keeps him hanging on every word you speak.
Appeal for Action	What should he do with the message?

Arresting the attention of your listeners is vital at the beginning of your message. It gives you and your speech a needed momentum. Besides, it keeps your listeners in the room with you. A story, a quote, a statistics, a joke…may be what you need to deploy. Some speakers bring props to the podium to demonstrate their points at the opening. After the terrorist attack on the twin-towers in New York, I attended the Presidential Prayer Breakfast in the following February. President George Bush was to speak at the breakfast. Unusually, I discovered a vacant seat on the top table. Immediately, I knew it was an integral part of the speech. President Bush, not known to be a fantastic speaker, made reference to the empty seat in his opening remarks. With the wounds of the attack still fresh, the drama of the vacant seat spoke eloquently of irreplaceable the victims were to their families and to their nations. There were many teary eyes in the audience.

Should you apologize at the opening of your speech? I think you should not, except in rare cases. What the listeners need at the beginning of a message is enthusiasm and not a dampening. They want to know what you know, see what you have seen and taste what you have tasted. Except they have been ambushed to listen to you, they are there to learn, to grow. Even if they are skeptics, they are there to listen to you fail or falter. Starting with apologies drain your energy and annoy your audience. Even in cases where I felt strongly that I needed to apologize, I did it about ten minutes into my speech – after I have got the audience roosting for me and for the message that I bore.

Should you greet people? Thanking them may be a great way to start, if that's part of your strategy. If not, go straight to implement your speech plan. You may do that in the middle of your speech, if necessary. There are some occasions where you are expected to follow some protocols at the opening. Please respect the tradition. If no such traditions exist, go straight into your speech.

Should you start with an opening prayer? Is that part of your plan? If not, you don't have to. Some do it to regain their composure, not because they want to. The same is true with reading the scriptures at the very beginning. To be sure, praying or reading the scriptures can be turn-offs your listeners do not need, especially if they are non-Christians.

You should move swiftly to creating interest. This is the time to identify the subject and, possibly, your qualification to handle it – especially if you are new to the audience. It is time to identify with their needs and speak their language. There is a problem to be solved. There is information they need. Let them know about the issues in a way that make them want to stay with you. Create interest; ignite a desire.

You have just ignited a desire; try and sustain it. Use stories of conquests. Cite examples of triumphs. You may talk about a coming doomsday if certain things are not done now. Talk about what is at stake. Sound convincing. Be passionate. How do you want them to feel? Happy? Sad? Confused? Whatever you want them to feel, demonstrate it, project it…till they feel that way. Let them feel like taking action – changing attitudes or moving in a different direction. Startle them with your new ideas. Make them eager to learn more.

Then, don't fail them. Go ahead and satisfy their hunger for action. Appeal for a verdict. Make the appeal consistent with your message. What action do you want them to take now? What do they need to do? What do they need to recall? Where do they need to go? At this point, the Holy Spirit is working in their minds, helping them sort out issues. In their minds, the listeners are considering if the new course of action would better that the one they are taking. There is a bit of doubt, even after such a beautiful speech. The enemy comes in – he actually never left – reminding them of what they stand to lose if they abandon their way of life.

Don't be afraid to be emotional. But don't overdo it. Don't be like a preacher that faked tears, just so he might persuade men to shed some too. The sad thing was that he did it from a heart of stone. He was one of those preaching the gospel out of deceit. He just wanted to make merchandise of the people.

Don't sell what you yourself would not buy. Don't ask the people to walk on the path you have not walked on or are not walking on. Don't sensationalise your closing. Don't turn a prophet, just so you might coerce people into the Kingdom. Let the Holy Spirit do his work after you have faithfully done yours.

Supposing no one indicates interest in making the decision on issues you have canvassed? Say, nobody indicates they want to give their lives to Jesus at the dinner you have been asked to speak in? This can be frustrating for a speaker, I know. But I have seen a lot to believe that not all disaster-looking evangelistic speeches are actually disastrous. I have heard of people who did not answer the altar call but had their lives changed at some meeting they attended.

• *Connecting with your audience*

If you cannot connect with the audience, you will never be able to get their listening attention and your appeal for action will fall on deaf ears.

To connect with your audience, do the following:
- Dress appropriately for the occasion
- Let your voice fill the room
- Modulate the rate and pitch of your voice.
- Be enthusiastic
- Maintain good eye contact. But refrain switching rapidly as if in a tennis match.
- Let your body language and gestures complement your words.
- Pronounce your words distinctly and

accurately
- Arrive on time and keep to the time allotted.
- Spend the time before your meeting getting to know your audience. They will pay back by giving your support during your speech.

In addition, take the VIP test, VIP being an acronym for Vulnerability, Identification and Personal Integrity.

Vulnerability: You don't have to reveal shocking details of your past mistakes. But you can talk about how a bad golfer or a cook you are – anything to let them know you are like a regular person. Contrary to the popular opinion, listeners connect more with the speakers that they think they have things in common with.

Identification: In incarnation, Jesus became us. Paul became all things to all men. Get the audience in your corner; tell them you are more like them. Before, during and after the speech, let the audience know you love them and are happy to be there. Break the ice. Talk one-on-one with some members of the audience before your speech. Shake hands. Let off your guard. Remember names and the proper way to pronounce them. Refer to a discussion with a member of the audience in the cause of your speech.

Personal Integrity: Public speaking is not much about techniques as it is about the heart. Audience soon reads into a shallow, empty presentation. Techniques may get you a foot in the door of men's heart, but only your credibility and personal integrity will keep you and your message in the room of their hearts. Be truthful in your assertions.

Here is wishing you a safe voyage in your next speech. But wait a minute. Don't make that speech until you have read the next and the final chapter. It is about the person who will write the report card of your speech.

ALL HAIL THE KING
OF COMMUNICATION

Will anyone contest who deserves the crown? We must put the crown where it belongs –on the head of the listener. And we have the Bible's approval for the coronation. In fact, long before communication experts began to speak on the need to focus attention on the listener to achieve effective communication, God had made his own pronouncement and had bestowed a crown on the listener's head.

Let's go back to where we started.

> *"Do not let any unwholesome talk come out of your mouths, but only what is helpful for building others up according to their needs, that it may benefit those who listen." Ephesians 4:29*

Every communication is out for one thing and one thing only – to benefit the listener. The listener is the king, deserving all the respect and the attention we can muster.

> *"But in your hearts revere Christ as Lord. Always be prepared to give an answer to everyone who asks you to give the reason for the hope that you have. But do this with gentleness and respect," 1 Peter 3:15*

Gentleness and respect? What honour on the king!

Getting To Know The King

This is one king you must research, finding out everything you can get on him. Like a doctor takes vital statistics of his patient, you too must take the Blood Pressure [**Bp**] of this listener-king. The more of him you know, the better equipped you are to get your message across to him. You will know how to gain an entrance into his court and how to conduct yourself therein. You will know how and when to appeal for a verdict.

Let's consider **Bp** as an acronym, meaning **B** – Background Information and **p** – Preoccupation Barriers.

For his *Background Information*, you want to answer the questions, Who, Where, What, and When and How about the listener. Who is he? Everything you can get hold on about him will be helpful - from gender to education; from social to economic; and from his attitudes to his choices and tastes. Where does he live? Where is he at on issues? Where is the best place to reach him? What does he know?

What doesn't he know? When is he best available to be reached? And how is the best way to reach him?

Then, you are concerned about his *Preoccupation Barriers*. You are interested in what experiences he has gone through that are worthy of note. What has happened to him lately? What are the obstacles militating against his acceptance of your message? What are his turn-ons and turn-offs? Turn-ons are things that motivate him and the turn-offs the things that demotivate him.

There is no need for you to be overwhelmed by this research. It's all in the service of the Great King to help the listener-king walk his path to freedom. Of course, the Holy Spirit comes in handy to help all the way, sometimes providing the missing links, sometimes prompting the needed areas of focus.

Adapting To The King

We have considered the issues of identification and building of common grounds with the listener. As the communicator, it's your responsibility to adapt to the listener, just like Jesus adapted to you. This calls for humility, just as Jesus demonstrated.

Your message should be packaged to suit him. From the Decision Model, you would know where he is at, spiritually, so that it can inform your expectation, your message and your closing.

You most adapt to him like Paul adapted to his listeners.

> *Even though I am free of the demands and expectations of everyone, I have voluntarily become a servant to any and all in order to reach a wide range of people: religious, nonreligious, meticulous moralists, loose-living immoralists, the defeated, the demoralized—whoever. I didn't take on their way of life. I kept my bearings in Christ—but I entered their world and tried to experience things from their point of view. I've become just about every sort of servant there is in my attempts to lead those I meet into a God-saved life. I did all this because of the Message. I didn't just want to talk about it; I wanted to be in on it!" 1 Corinthians 9:19-23 [MSG]*

Whatever you do, celebrate the listener-king, just so you might bring him to the Great King. Endeavour to build him up according to his needs and with all gentleness and respect.

BIBLIOGRAPHY

Landa Cope, *Clearly Communicating Christ: Breaking down barriers to effective communication:* (YWAM Publishing; July, 1996)

George Ninan and Anita E. Mellot, Who *is listening? What you need to know about communication and the gospel* (Atlanta, Haggai Institute for advanced leadership training, 2002)

John Haggai, *Lead On: Leadership that endures in a changing world* (Texas, World Books page, 1986)

David J. Hesselgrave, Communicating Christ Cross-Culturally, Second Edition (Zondervan, May 30, 1991)

Douglas Shaw, Sharing Jesus: Communicating Christ Effectively (Gospel Light Publications; Manual edition, January, 1999)

Richard E. Porter & Larry A. Samovar, *Intercultural Communication: A Reader* (Belmont, California: Wordsworth Publishing Company, 1988)

Bill Hybels and Mark Mittelsberg, *Becoming a contagious Christian* (Zondervan: May 2, 1996)